Hooked On Heartbreak

For more information about related books and resources:

BennettTwins.Com

Hooked On Heartbreak

A Strategic Guide To Understand and Break Your Addiction To A Toxic Ex Or Partner

David Bennett and Jonathan Bennett

Theta Hill Press

Lancaster, Ohio

thetahillpress.com

Copyright Notice

All rights are reserved. No part of this publication may be reproduced, stored in a retrieval system or transmitted in any form or by any means, electronic, mechanical, photocopying, recording or otherwise, without prior permission.

Copyright © 2023 Theta Hill Press

ISBN: 979-8-9887090-0-8

Important Disclaimer (Yes Read This)

The information in this book is intended as an educational aid only. No information contained in this book should be construed as medical or psychological advice, counseling, diagnosis, or treatment. The authors are coaches, hypnotists, and writers sharing their personal experiences.

Readers should consult appropriate health professionals on any matter relating to their health and well-being, including mental health, and before starting any health or self-improvement program.

If you are in a relationship situation that places you, or someone you love, in any sort of danger or harm, make sure you are in a place and position of safety before implementing any of the strategies outlined in this book. Please read this book only if you can do so safely.

If you are in danger from someone abusive, please contact local emergency authorities immediately. If you need any sort of non-emergency assistance, please contact local agencies dedicated to making sure your physical, financial, emotional, and safety needs can be properly met.

Contents

Introduction: Why I'm Writing This Book	9
Chapter 1: Let's Talk About Hypnosis For A Minute	16
Chapter 2: Toxic Partner Story Time: Maria	24
Chapter 3: Toxic Partner Story Time: Rachel	32
Chapter 4: Toxic Partner Story Time: Mark	36
Chapter 5: What Does It Mean To Be Toxic Anyway?	42
Chapter 6: Are You *Really* Addicted?	49
Chapter 7: You're Used To Being You	59
Chapter 8: Your Three Brains	66
Chapter 9: Short-Term Infatuation's Brain Drain	74
Chapter 10: Your Brain Is In It For The Long Haul	87
Chapter 11: Trauma Bonding 1: Intermittent Rewards and Punishments	93
Chapter 12: Trauma Bonding 2: What Is Trauma?	102
Chapter 13: Trauma Bonding 3: Survival Mode	111
Chapter 14: Trauma Bonding 4 Turning Toxic Too	115
Chapter 15: Trauma Bonding 5: Your Faulty Frontal Lobe	119
Chapter 16: So That's A Lot Of Bad News	126
Chapter 17: Take Responsibility	129
Chapter 18: Now Forgive Yourself	135

Chapter 19: Correcting Cranial Chemistry	140
Chapter 20: Breaking The Bonds	147
Chapter 21: Re-Wiring Your Brain	151
Chapter 22: The 7-Step Creation Protocol	155
Chapter 23: The Confidence-Accomplishment Spiral	167
Chapter 24: Restoring Balance	170
Chapter 25: Limit Access	182
Chapter 26: Saying "No" And Basic Boundaries	188
Chapter 27: This Too Shall Pass	194
Chapter 28: The "Unnamed Clothing Company Text Test"	198
Chapter 29: What About Dating?	203
Chapter 30: Gratitude	208
Chapter 31: Future Deeper Work Part 1: Time, Support, And Integration	212
Chapter 32: Future Deeper Work Part 2: Letting Go	216
Chapter 33: Hoping For The Best	221
Chapter 34: Putting It All Together	225
Appendix A: Glossary Of Toxic Manipulation Tactics	227
Appendix B: Who We Are	241
Appendix C: More Support and Resources	245
Appendix D: References	250

Invictus

Out of the night that covers me,
Black as the Pit from pole to pole,
I thank whatever gods may be
For my unconquerable soul.

In the fell clutch of circumstance
I have not winced nor cried aloud.
Under the bludgeonings of chance
My head is bloody, but unbowed.

Beyond this place of wrath and tears
Looms but the Horror of the shade,
And yet the menace of the years
Finds, and shall find, me unafraid.

It matters not how strait the gate,
How charged with punishments the scroll,
I am the master of my fate:
I am the captain of my soul.

William Ernest Henley (1875)

INTRODUCTION

WHY I'M WRITING THIS BOOK

I've always been interested in dating and relationships. I wrote my first "work" on dating and relationships in 1994. I was a sophomore in high school, and I wrote an essay reflecting on my fledgling entrance into the realm of love, including offering advice on how to win over potential dates and make relationships last.

While I still have many of my English essays from that time, I never got that one back from the teacher. I'm sure much of what I wrote was ridiculous and naive, and I'm grateful Mrs. Wiggins gave me an "A" on it despite that. Who knows, maybe she saved it and applied my advice, but I highly doubt it.

Since that time, Jonathan and I have worked as dating coaches. Part of our work was partnering with local matchmakers, helping their clients connect better with their matches and dates. In that time, we even got chances to audition for some potential dating reality shows, but sadly they never materialized.

During this time, I also studied hypnosis and received my certification to practice. In 2020, I got on TikTok. I considered myself officially done with the field of dating and relationships, and was focusing more on hypnosis, coaching, and self-growth.

I believe that to live a fulfilled life, you must focus on your physical health, emotional health, spiritual health, and social health. As a part of this last domain, I produced TikTok content on relationships occasionally.

While my initial content did fairly well, I really took off in popularity when I started talking about relationships, particularly toxic ones and recovering from them.

I had always known relationships were a very tricky issue for most people. I had seen many relationships fail spectacularly, among my friends, acquaintances, and even my own. But, I wasn't prepared for the sheer number of people who were presently stuck in toxic relationships or struggling to get over a toxic ex. It was, and is, an epidemic, that many people are ashamed to acknowledge and talk about.

When I started shifting some of my content in this direction, I started to go viral quickly. My TikTok videos on disempowering and standing up to toxic people got millions of views and thousands of comments. My videos on love addiction went even more viral, with one reaching 4.5 million views (and an additional two million when I later re-posted it).

I honestly was amazed how many people were dealing with an addiction to toxic partners, both currently, and as exes.

This got me thinking a lot about the "whys" and "hows" of toxic relationships. Fortunately, my professional and educational background allowed me to make sense of it, particularly the way I understand the brain and hypnosis.

I go "live" on TikTok a lot, and I almost always get the same repeated questions related to toxic relationships, and they usually involve some element of "addiction" to someone toxic.

I put "addiction" in quotes simply because you won't find "addiction to someone toxic" in any DSM (Diagnostic and Statistical Manual) used to diagnose mental disorders.

However, I do believe that you can become addicted to someone. I also believe that even falling in love is at least "addiction-like," as do many researchers (1).

This book is an attempt to provide answers for those who are addicted to toxic people, as well as their loved ones and therapists or coaches (more on this in a moment).

Just know that if you are addicted to a toxic ex, or even a toxic partner, you're not alone. Millions of people just like you have seen my social media content, and many of these people regularly visit my live events to share their stories and concerns.

I have found myself struggling to get over exes that weren't good for me as well. Every one of my friends, regardless of gender, has gone through the same thing. Some are still stuck on toxic exes, years and even decades later.

The goal of this book is to help you understand the addiction you have to someone toxic: how it started, why it is addictive in nature, what is keeping you addicted, and how to heal from it.

As you read this book, including the stories and chapters about the signs of addiction and brain chemistry changes, things will start to make sense.

You'll understand why you keep going back to someone toxic, even if you know they are bad for you. You'll discover why nobody else seems as exciting and attractive as your toxic partner or ex, even if this new potential date is nice, kind, and good for you. You'll learn why you have become emotionally reactive, and perhaps are even developing toxic habits yourself. You'll gain these insights and many more.

My desire is to help you go from someone whose life is consumed by someone toxic, to reach a point where you view them neutrally – neither excited to see them, nor angrily obsessed with hating them.

By the time you are done with this book, I hope you are on the path of filling your head with good things, good experiences, and good people who aren't that toxic person who now consumes your mind.

I am also writing this book with healers, friends, and family members in mind. This book is just as useful for therapists, coaches, and support groups. As you'll see repeatedly in various chapters, people addicted to someone toxic rarely see the extent of the damage that is happening to them.

Like other addicts, they minimize consequences, cover up for their toxic partners, and refuse to take responsibility for their own role in the relationship. Because of this, it's often up to family and community members to help them not only see the destructive nature of their toxic relationship and addiction, but also to get them help.

I hope you find this book insightful and helpful. If you're reading this, that means you are open to change and ready to begin a healing journey. This puts you way ahead of most people and means you have grown stronger and more powerful than you used to be.

I fully believe that you're capable of overcoming your addiction to your toxic ex or partner, and healing and getting your life back. I have seen thousands of people do it, and their only regret is that they didn't start the process sooner.

I included the "Invictus" poem before this chapter because it eloquently expresses the ability of humans to endure the most difficult of situations and emerge from them. If you're reading this, then it means that you're capable of doing this as well.

At this point, you may not believe me, that someone like you is capable of healing, because of possible shame you have related to your addiction to someone toxic. However, I invite you to begin your healing journey today, even if you feel ridiculous, stupid, or weak. As you'll see by reading this book, you aren't any of those things.

I promise you aren't alone, and you aren't in "too deep" to heal! I've worked with many clients who felt the way you do. Some became involved in morally questionable activities because of their toxic partner. Others abandoned friendships and family connections or put their children's safety in jeopardy. Some were in healthy relationships and struggled with feelings of deep attraction to a toxic ex. They even felt tempted to cheat on their current partner with their toxic ex.

So, no matter what shame or unworthiness you may be feeling, please stick around and keep reading.

You may have noticed this book is written by two people, but uses the "I" perspective. I, David Bennett, am the primary author, but my twin brother Jonathan and I edit and rewrite for each other, so we give each other credit. It's kind of like a Lennon-McCartney thing, only we get along better than John and Paul did (this is a Beatles reference for all you younger folks).

You may wonder who I am, and what my role is in the "toxic relationship" space. Along with my twin brother, I'm a hypnotist, coach, and produce content on social media about self-growth, which includes relationship content, since this is an important aspect of self-growth.

I raise awareness, provide support, and share research. I work with clients in a variety of areas related to self-improvement, providing clients with support, accountability, coaching, and hypnosis to help them change their mindset, heal, and replace unhealthy habits and patterns with new ones.

I do not provide therapy or treat any sort of mental illness, but I do collaborate and coordinate with therapists when this is needed.

Soon, I'm going to outline the nature of your addiction to someone toxic: how it began, how it is maintained, and how to break the addiction. However, first I'm going to explain a foundational element of this book and share a few stories you'll likely relate to.

Chapter 1

Let's Talk About Hypnosis For A Minute

Why is a hypnotist writing a book about getting over a toxic partner or ex? That's a great question!

Most people think of hypnosis in a few ways. A lot of people imagine a flamboyantly dressed hypnotist getting people to do funny things on stage. This is absolutely hypnosis.

Another popular understanding is a hypnotist using a swinging pocket watch to make someone "sleepy" and send them into a trance. Yes, this is hypnosis as well.

Finally, a good chunk of people believe it is about secret mind control. And, yes, that is a form of hypnosis. I promise I'm not using that here (or *am I??*). Sorry, that's just a little hypnosis humor. I promise the only hypnosis I'm going to do in this book is to undo the hypnosis your toxic ex or partner has done on you.

All these definitions of hypnosis actually relate to why you get into toxic relationships, why you stay in them, and also why you have trouble getting over a toxic ex.

I define hypnosis like this: "a special way of paying attention that stimulates your unconscious imagination to generate a new internal reality of emotions and beliefs that is stronger than the old internal reality of emotions and beliefs, which causes you to take action, thus changing your external reality."

In plain English, this means that hypnosis is anything that really gets your attention at a deep level, and causes you to make significant changes based on that.

By this definition, a charming, flirtatious date who is so attractive that you can't stop thinking about them is hypnotizing you. Also, a comment on social media by someone who really aggravates you and causes you to think about the argument all day, and reply quickly and immediately, even if you are busy doing other things, is hypnotizing you.

The high-sugar cereal box with bright colors and a prize inside is hypnotizing you both through the advertising and the high-sugar content.

And, your ex (or current partner) has likely hypnotized you throughout the entire process of your relationship, including their charm and grand promises at the beginning, as well as the intermittent rewards and punishments throughout the relationship (we'll discuss this later).

In the same way, since a form of hypnosis got you into this mess, a form of hypnosis can get you out.

I've mentioned the "unconscious" when defining hypnosis, so let me explain this further.

Hypnotists like me divide your mind into the "conscious mind" and "unconscious mind." I use the term "unconscious mind" as a synonym for "subconscious." I'm mentioning this, since you may have heard that term instead.

This isn't about brain structures per se, although certain structures could be considered more "unconscious" than others (like the brain stem and limbic structures, which I'll discuss later).

This conscious and unconscious division is descriptive of the processing happening in your mind. Your conscious mind consists of the thoughts and sensations that you are aware of. Unless you're just skimming through this part of the book right now, you're likely engaging your conscious mind.

It's that part of you that is logical, makes sense, is structured, and vocalizes what you want. It's who you wish you were, and who you likely present yourself as on social media. It is largely synonymous with "the ego."

Your unconscious mind is the part of you that is usually outside of your conscious awareness. Your unconscious mind includes highly unconscious processes like your heartbeat, automatic breathing, and many bodily operations that happen all the time that you aren't even aware of.

But, it also includes things that you may be aware of at times, or even fuzzily aware of. This includes things like motivations, feelings, cravings, bodily sensations, attraction preferences, addictions, habits, trauma responses, emotional reactivity, deep and dark desires, innate desires (like to reproduce, mother a child, or seek pleasure), and even things you may have learned in childhood before you were consciously aware.

At the end of the day, your unconscious mind wants to survive, feel good, avoid feeling bad, and maintain familiarity. It wants familiarity at all costs because your unconscious mind isn't very logical, so it conflates familiarity with safety. So, if you have done something for a long time, even if you wish you didn't do it, your unconscious mind will likely keep doing it.

This is why when you go to start a new habit, your unconscious mind will resist. You'll get sick. You'll feel bad. You'll suddenly get "busy." You'll convince yourself it's better to give up than try harder. You'll convince yourself the horrible situation you're in isn't really that bad after all. You may have experienced many of these unconscious urgings when you tried to leave your toxic partner.

Here is a humorous illustration of the battle between the conscious mind and the unconscious mind. In parenthesis, I'll label the differences. This is where I want to introduce an important rule in hypnosis: *the unconscious mind always wins in the end*. By this, I mean that you'll usually default to what you unconsciously want, even if you consciously want to do something different. So, now to the story…

You just finished watching a TikTok on not being reactive and you tell yourself, "I need to be less reactive" (conscious). Right after you watch it, your partner yells at you to stop wasting your time on "that stupid app," and you get so furious that you tell yourself that you'll try the whole "less reactive thing" next time (unconscious – old habits, familiarity). So, you scream back at them (unconscious - reactivity). You calm down in a few hours, and since it's getting late in the evening, you decide that you have had enough, so you force yourself to go to bed (conscious).

You tell yourself you're going to wake up early at 7:30 AM so you have enough time to get to work early and call a lawyer about a divorce and start looking for your own place (conscious). However, you're so rattled by the contentious exchange earlier, you can't fall asleep (unconscious).

The next morning, the alarm goes off and you're just so exhausted, you hit snooze (unconscious – habit, feelings, motivation).

You're rushing out the door and your partner makes a snide comment, so you yell at them for five minutes (unconscious – reactivity, habit, trauma response).

You're frazzled on the way to work and are trying to text-fight with them while driving, even though it's dangerous (unconscious – reactivity, habit).

You get to work, almost late, and your boss already has work for you to do. You decide you'll call the lawyer on your break (conscious). However, you're so exhausted on your break, and you see a co-worker brought donuts, so you eat a few of them and then scroll on social media (unconscious – cravings, habits). When your co-worker comes in, you catch up on the recent gossip in the office (unconscious – habits, instant reward).

Your co-worker asks about your relationship. You say you really need to do something about that (conscious). They ask some deeper questions, and you freeze and emotionally shut down, and the situation gets awkward (unconscious – trauma response). Soon after this interaction, you have a stomach ache (unconscious – bodily sensation).

Your break is over, and you tell yourself you'll call the lawyer "right after work" (conscious).

As the end of work approaches, you feel exhausted. It's been a long day! Plus, you just didn't "have the time" today. "It's been so busy!" you exclaim, even though you had plenty of time to scroll and play phone games to avoid doing work duties (unconscious – habits, addictions).

As your workday unwinds, your partner texts you something to provoke you, and you furiously text them for the last ten minutes of work (unconscious – addiction, emotional reactivity).

You get home and the lawyer's office is closed. Plus, your partner was being a little nicer to you during dinner, so you conclude that maybe it would just be easier to stay (unconscious – habits, emotions, familiarity).

As you can see, most of what we do isn't dictated by our conscious minds. It's dictated by our unconscious minds. You may have never thought of things this way until you read this chapter.

This is how deeply unconscious many of your behaviors are. Despite conscious goals that align with your higher purpose, you end up giving in to your unconscious mind.

Unfortunately, solutions to unconscious problems require access to the unconscious mind, but most of our attempts at solutions are conscious in nature. It's why simply talking about your problems rarely helps you (think of how much you have vented about your toxic partner to your friends). It's also why sheer "willpower" often doesn't work.

This is why hypnosis and hypnotic interventions are so useful. They work at an unconscious level, and that is why the interventions I'm going to discuss later in this book have been so helpful for those who have used them.

I added this chapter because my understanding of the unconscious and conscious will permeate this book, so starting with it is a good idea.

Before I get into the nuts and bolts of understanding your addiction to someone toxic, I want to share a few stories that you can likely relate to.

I've worked with many clients who are addicted to someone toxic, and have helped them change their mindsets, heal, and develop the confidence to make major life changes.

I provide support and accountability so they can break their addictions to an ex or partner. I have done some of this work on TikTok itself, through live interactions, but worked with others in my coaching practice.

These stories are based on thousands of people I've helped, professionally and personally, and are used with their consent. I've changed names and details, and combined and conflated stories, to make them totally anonymous. No person in any of the following stories represents any particular individual.

It doesn't even matter anyway, because the stories I'll tell you are so common that they likely describe what you're going through (or what your loved one or client is facing).

Chapter 2

Toxic Partner Story Time: Maria

Maria started out believing Scott was the "love of her life." He came on very strong. He was charming, good-looking, and knew exactly what to say to Maria, who was recently divorced.

Maria believed she would never fall in love again after her divorce. Her ex-husband had checked out of the relationship and ended up being unfaithful. Her kids were grown, and she felt very alone after the divorce.

She met Scott on a dating app, and she was initially shocked that a guy who looked as good as he did would match with her, since her last relationship didn't exactly make her feel desirable.

They started texting and went on a first date. He was so cute and charismatic that she felt alive again for the first time since her divorce. She gushed to her friends, who jokingly said Maria was back in middle school again.

After the second date, Scott "innocently" suggested that Maria go back to his place to meet his dog, since they had discussed their mutual love of animals on their dates. "One thing led to another," and despite Maria pledging to herself she would never sleep with a guy before they knew each other for at least three months, they slept together.

"Scott seemed different," she told me, so breaking her rule was okay.

The passion was significant, and Maria found herself hooked on Scott on many levels.

They went on a third date a week later, meeting for a nice dinner. Scott was lingering in the restaurant waiting area as Maria was running a few minutes late.

"Traffic was so heavy, and it was pouring down rain! I'm so sorry I'm a few minutes late," she said.

Scott tensed up and barely said a word for the next ten minutes. He lashed out at the hostess.

"Why isn't there a table open yet?" He grumbled. "You said '20 minutes' and it's been nearly a half hour!"

Maria was taken aback, but Scott quickly pointed out that he only talked like that because he wanted the best possible date experience for Maria.

At some level, that excited Maria because her ex-husband never cared enough to go on a date, let alone make sure the evening was perfect. Scott's passion was impressive.

However, throughout the date, Scott kept harping on her about being late, and started comparing her to "dumb exes" who were "always" late. He played the comments off as jokes, but Maria felt uneasy.

However, once the food came, he was in a good mood again and making her feel nice. He invited her to his home after dinner, and Maria was craving the passion, so she agreed.

Within a few weeks, Scott mentioned that he was getting kicked out of his apartment. "It was totally unfair," he told her. His neighbor was parking in the wrong space, like he always did, and Scott confronted him about following the rules.

The neighbor got upset, and Scott ended up defending himself. The neighbor called the cops and Scott got arrested. It was a "giant mix up" and the apartment manager had it out for Scott for months. So, now Scott was going to be homeless.

Scott said, "you know, it's crazy…nah…you wouldn't even consider it…."

"What?" Maria asked.

"Well, you and I have this deep connection, so maybe I can stay with you. I would obviously pay rent, and do my part to clean and fix up the place. I'd leave anytime you needed me to. You told me you could use the money and 'felt alone' in your place since your divorce."

Before she knew it, Scott was moving in, even though they barely knew each other. Maria's friends were skeptical, but she saw it as a sign they were meant to be, and something that would happen in a romance movie.

After he moved in, Scott's life was filled with a series of "mix-ups" and "misunderstandings" with all kinds of people.

She found out that his ex-wife had a restraining order against him. His kids didn't talk to him. His co-workers wouldn't ever hang out with him.

Scott was also late on rent for the first month, but again, it was a big misunderstanding. He had to pay some fees related to the fight he got into at the apartment.

He couldn't be expected to pay his rent this month, he reasoned, because Maria knew beforehand he would have those fees. Scott implied Maria was insensitive for even asking for rent after knowing he had to fight the injustice related to his arrest.

Scott also started flying off the handle more at home. He would get angry easily, and yell and scream. After about an hour, he would calm down, have a few beers or a snack, and then he'd be back to "normal."

By the time night came, he was ready for the passionate, exciting romance that Maria craved as well.

Maria's friends and family started to voice concerns. She hadn't been coming to family gatherings. Every time her friends reached out to meet, she had some flimsy excuse. She didn't have the heart to tell them that it was because if she left the house too much, Scott would pout and get upset.

Maria didn't necessarily see this as a bad thing: she reasoned that Scott just loved her so much that he wanted to spend his free time with her.

After about six months, Scott was in a bad mood more than he was in a good mood. He paid rent sporadically, but Maria stopped asking for it because he would get angry if she brought it up.

The passion stopped most nights, unless Scott was really in the mood, and at times he pressured Maria into sex even if she was tired or sick.

Scott started leaving the house a lot more often, but wouldn't allow Maria to leave.

One night, Maria's friend called her to tell her that she saw Scott at a local bar with another woman. Maria confronted Scott about it, and they got into a massive screaming match. Scott insisted she was just a friend, and it was obviously an attempt by Maria's friend to sabotage their relationship.

"See, I was right! This is why I didn't want you hanging out with her!" Scott exclaimed with a red face.

Maria spent the night crying. Scott woke up and was deeply apologetic. He was so sorry for the misunderstanding and understood why Maria was upset. He promised he would change. This promise made her feel a sense of relief.

But just a few days later, everything was back to "normal." Scott had lost his job a few weeks earlier because he threatened a co-worker. He just got around to telling Maria, and this meant that she now was fully supporting Scott, who seemed very happy to just sit around most of the day and watch TV.

Maria started to realize her relationship with Scott was taking a toll on her mental health. She suggested they go to counseling. Scott thought that was a horrible idea and refused to go, and discouraged Maria from going.

After a year of this, Maria didn't recognize the person she had become. She had no friends, barely left the house, and was spending all day dealing with Scott in some way. She had gained 30 pounds as well.

She rarely had any money because Scott wouldn't work, and she was even paying to deal with Scott's legal fees resulting from his destructive behavior.

She was constantly text-fighting with him while she was at work. She was frazzled and looked ten years older than her actual age. She finally told Scott he had to leave.

He threw a fit, yelled, and screamed. He blamed Maria for their relationship breakdown, but reluctantly left.

Maria found herself missing Scott a lot. She woke up thinking about him and was constantly checking his social media for any signs he had moved on. Whenever she saw that Scott was doing something social, she was simultaneously furious and missing his touch.

He reached out to her after a few weeks with the amazingly charming text, "miss u. Meet?" Maria's friends pointed out the lack of effort in that text, but as much as she hated to admit it, she missed him. So, she agreed to meet.

Scott said he had learned his lesson and had done some serious reflecting. He even said that he had cried because he missed her so much. That impressed Maria tremendously.

They met up, and Scott seemed genuinely sorry. They ended up sleeping together that night, and everything felt so good and familiar.

The next day, as Maria was getting up and Scott was asleep, his phone rang. Maria noticed a woman's name on it. She confronted Scott about the woman. He said it was just his cousin who needed help moving.

Maria went to the bathroom and looked up on Facebook the name she had thought she had seen. Getting a strange feeling, she sent the photo to her friend. Her friend confirmed that this was the woman she had seen Scott with at the bar.

Maria confronted Scott with this information, and he stormed out, as he yelled and screamed at Maria for her suspicion, implying he only cheated to begin with because she never trusted him.

By the time Maria came to me, Scott had moved on multiple times, and had posted photos on social media with a host of different women, but Maria was still stuck on him. She stalked his social media daily, brought him up in nearly every conversation, and even sabotaged a few first dates with other guys by talking about him constantly.

She tried to find a few new guys attractive, but none of them had the charm, excitement, and looks of Scott.

As time passed, she even felt that maybe she unfairly judged Scott, and was secretly hoping that he might reach out to her and see how she was doing.

However, after a few months, she noticed Scott was living with a different woman who was glowing with excitement that she was officially in a relationship with him.

Chapter 3

Toxic Partner Story Time: Rachel

Rachel was in her mid-20s and had been with her boyfriend since high school. She started coming on my TikTok lives because she started to believe she was going crazy.

Her boyfriend Tyler had cheated on her a few times. Each time, she reluctantly agreed to go back to him because, as she said, "I felt bad, because he can't make it without someone like me in his life."

Tyler had a rough upbringing. His dad was never in his life, and his mom had addiction issues. He was in foster care for major periods in his life.

In school, Tyler was a quiet, cute kid, who was the class rebel. There was something about his style that made Rachel intrigued by him. He wasn't overtly rebellious. He was very quiet, and just did his own thing. His grades were below-average, and he made funny comments in class that angered uptight teachers.

Rachel was a "good kid," who was quiet and got decent grades. Her parents weren't pleased that she was dating Tyler, and initially objected. She found herself lying to them often and sneaking out to see him.

On their first date, which was hanging out after school while Rachel's parents thought she was at band practice, they talked for hours. By the time she came onto my TikTok live events, Tyler felt so familiar to her. He was the first guy who ever gave her any attention. Rachel was weirdly attracted to Tyler but also felt sorry for him.

"Fixing" Tyler was a full-time job. Rachel often told her family that nobody understood Tyler but her, and one time when Tyler thought she might break up with him, he implied he might do something extreme to harm himself.

She was not only deeply in love with Tyler, but she believed she was living a sort of tragic romance novel. She wanted to be there through all of Tyler's brokenness and woundedness. This idea made her mind come alive. It was like something out of an art movie, and she took pride in this, even looking at "normal," more stable, relationships with scorn.

They fought constantly while in high school. Rachel was college-bound, while Tyler didn't do much of anything except smoke weed, play video games, and "hang out."

Rachel wanted to go to college a few hours away and study to be an architect, a childhood dream of hers. However, Tyler didn't want her to go. He wouldn't be able to afford a place in a college town, and Rachel had no way of getting a place to live with him. Her parents were opposed to them dating, so there was no way they would pay for it.

Rachel decided to stay in her hometown and get into a nursing program instead, even though she hated nursing.

As soon as she graduated from college, she found a job, got a place, and Tyler moved in immediately. A big source of fighting was that Tyler wouldn't work. He always had an excuse.

However, she threatened to leave him, so he did get a retail job. Tyler met a woman there whom he messaged all the time on Snapchat. Rachel suspected it was happening for months, but never really pushed it.

Soon, Rachel was pressuring Tyler for marriage, and believed that if she could just get him to propose, he'd finally grow up and mature.

The reason for her meeting with me was that Tyler was being very sketchy with his phone and social media.

Tyler demanded that Rachel show him her social media activity, but he refused to reciprocate. Rachel knew he had trust issues from his childhood, so she reluctantly accepted this.

However, she had glanced over and seen that he was clearly messaging a girl, and it was likely the woman from work.

Originally, she was meeting with me to figure out how to better understand Tyler's behavior, and to get him to admit that he was indeed cheating so she could fix the relationship and marry him.

While my background in psychology, hypnosis, and communication strategies allowed me to help her do that, the path I eventually helped steer her down was understanding that she deserved way better than this.

Rachel had been with Tyler for eight years, and the thought of not being with him seemed so weird. So, rather than questioning whether she should leave Tyler, she only thought about finding ways to cope, and fix Tyler. However, by her own admission, none of that ever worked.

She was losing her mind, constantly worrying about what was on Tyler's phone, and yet feeling shame for not trusting him.

She couldn't focus most of the day worrying about what Tyler was doing. It was consuming her life.

The "crap hit the fan" when Tyler lost his job, and she had to take extra shifts to cover the missing income, only to find out that he was spending his free time not only texting his now ex-coworker, but also sleeping with her.

Chapter 4

Toxic Partner Story Time: Mark

Mark was a firefighter and very successful in many ways. He was a nice guy, had a great job, and was active in his community.

Mark met a woman named Christy while he was at a local bar one night. She was partying with friends and sat next to him. She was very flirtatious and physically beautiful. Mark was a little shocked that a woman this pretty would even talk to him, as she was "out of his league."

He got her number and texted her the next day. She gave him short texts, and took a long time to respond, but Mark was very enamored.

Over the next few months, Mark met up with her, and they would go out and party. Sometimes, they had dinner together. On some occasions, Mark even paid for drinks for all her friends. Christy often got so drunk that she would hang all over other guys at the bar.

After one night when she behaved extremely inappropriately, Mark got jealous and brought it up. She insisted it was "no big deal" and he was just being insecure. She was just flirty and fun! That was just "who she was."

Mark finally pressed her for some commitment, and while she was reluctant, she agreed. Within a month, she had moved into Mark's house.

As they started seeing more of each other, Mark learned that Christy had been involved with a guy named Steve. Steve was manipulative and toxic. Christy constantly trashed Steve and described him as a very bad person who manipulated her.

However, Christy admitted she had seen Steve as recently as a few days before Mark had asked her to commit.

She assured Mark it was no big deal, and she just happened to run into him at a local coffee shop. They sat and talked about a few insignificant things, and then both were on their way.

However, something seemed off to Mark. He noticed on Instagram that Christy had liked every one of Steve's recent photos and even made some very positive comments about him on those posts.

If she hated him so much, then why was she complimenting him on Instagram?

Christy said she was just "being nice," and suggested Mark shouldn't police her behavior, since he was acting in a toxic way. She then changed the subject. But she said she would stop following Steve if it would make Mark feel better.

Mark still had weird gut feelings about Christy and Steve. He noticed that Steve went off Instagram suddenly. However, after he checked from a friend's account, he realized Steve had blocked him, even though Steve had never met Mark. His friend also noticed that Christy was still following Steve and engaging his posts.

One night when Mark and Christy were intimate, he didn't use protection, and she got pregnant. Mark was scared, but also oddly excited in a way. He figured this may be just what Christy needed to finally settle down and devote herself to him the way he did to her.

However, things just got weirder. She started backing away and suggested that maybe Mark and her weren't right for each other. While she wanted to be a mother and was going to have the baby, Mark was just "too much."

She couldn't see why Mark cared that she was still friends with her toxic ex. She reminded Mark that she had already told him that she didn't like Steve "that way," and lamented that Mark's insecurity was becoming a huge turn-off.

Christy also was hiding her phone a lot, and one night Mark noticed she was messaging Steve. When he glanced over, he saw a bunch of messages, and what he thought was a heart emoji. Mark became upset and accused her of cheating on him with Steve.

"Steve is trying to come back into my life and I'm handling it!" she said angrily when Mark asked about it. "Do you want me to just let him think he can come back?"

When Mark asked to see the exchange so he could support her in "handling" Steve, she got angry and blamed Mark for not trusting her.

"This is what I'm talking about Mark!" she screamed. "I told you that I'll handle it!"

When Mark reached out to me, he thought he was going crazy. Like most clients who reach out to me for issues like this, Mark's main concern was figuring out how to better love and support Christy rather than handle their clearly toxic situation.

But Christy had no desire to fix anything. The more Mark pushed to get help to repair their relationship, the more she became angry and distant.

Finally, she told Mark she was moving out because he was stressing her out constantly. She said she was going to move in with her cousin. Mark was sad, but at least her cousin was a decent person, and she would care for Christy, who was further along in her pregnancy.

Mark was still desperate to fix the relationship and get Christy to see how important it was to remain with him, at the very least for the baby.

However, soon Mark found out that Christy wasn't living with her cousin, but was instead living with Steve.

Mark felt betrayed, but still deeply loved Christy. Not only was he the father of their unborn child (at least as far as he knew), but he felt like he could never do better than Christy.

He thought about her constantly and found himself creating social media accounts to track her and Steve. He was sending walls of text trying to convince her to come back to him.

After having a major fight with Steve where he got abusive, Christy agreed to meet with Mark. She told Mark that she could let him into her life as the father, but she wasn't sure about a romantic relationship. She just didn't feel like Mark was right for her, and that he was "too good for her."

Mark was devastated, but he was happy to just have any relationship with her, and immediately pressed her to meet again, and to resume texting "for the baby's sake."

Christy reluctantly agreed that she could do this, but she wasn't going to move out from Steve's place.

Like a heroin addict who has just gotten a fix, Mark was feeling good about the fact that he could now text Christy again semi-regularly and even see her, even if she was living with Steve.

He constantly defended Christy's actions, explaining that he was "a lot" to deal with at times, and that she had only cheated on him and moved in with Steve because of her own trauma and addiction to Steve.

"Steve is controlling her, and she is being tricked," he told himself (and me). He convinced himself that over time he might even be able to convince Christy to see the light and realize the error of her ways, and they could be a happy family together. He believed the solution was to be there for Christy even more than before, even if she was openly dating Steve.

Chapter 5

What Does It Mean To Be "Toxic" Anyway?

Just visit social media for even a few minutes, and you'll see the word "toxic" thrown around almost immediately. The term has appeared in many of my videos and posts.

Believe it or not, I'm not a big fan of the term "toxic." For one, there is no scientific consensus related to that term, so it can mean virtually anything and everything. Second, it is often used as a label to criticize someone that we simply just don't like.

And, it's a label, and like all labels, it's not often helpful for growth. Calling someone "toxic" is like calling someone a "loser." By labeling them with that term, it can encourage them to embrace the traits of the label and keep them stuck in that unhelpful state.

However, I nonetheless reluctantly use the term, because it is used so much in popular culture and on social media.

Another term I dislike even more is the label "narcissist." Like the term "toxic" it gets thrown around so much that it has become nearly meaningless. It too is often used to describe people that may simply just be common jerks or people whom we just don't like.

There is an actual condition called "narcissistic personality disorder," which is a serious personality disorder. It is a disorder that affects perhaps as little as 0.5% of the population, and as high as 5% (2).

NPD is a clinically defined disorder, a part of the Cluster B personality disorders, as classified by the DSM-V. This cluster includes similar personality disorders, like "borderline personality disorder," which impacts women more than men, and is in many ways similar to NPD. Research shows BPD may be slightly more common than NPD.

The term "narcissist" doesn't necessarily mean someone is clinically diagnosed with NPD or BPD, even among psychologists and scientists. It can be used for those who exhibit extreme self-centeredness.

Plus, there is the issue that all of us are self-centered in some way, as that is necessary for survival in many cases. In fact, if you spend any time on TikTok, many of the people always talking about how their exes are narcissists often have many of the same self-centered traits as their ex.

My point is that throwing around the terms "toxic" and "narcissist" makes both terms lose their meaning, and can make it harder for people to identify genuinely toxic people and narcissists.

So, based on my research, I define a "narcissist" as someone whose self-centered behaviors are causing very significant emotional, social, or physical problems in their life, or the lives of those close to them, combined with a lack of awareness that their behaviors are playing a role in these problems.

There are two types of narcissists: grandiose and vulnerable (sometimes called "covert").

Grandiose narcissists are what we think of as classical narcissists. These individuals are bombastic, bold, charming, calculating, and focus on being successful at what they do at all costs. These are the politicians, celebrities, and romantic "players." They often care a lot about their physical appearance (and flaunt it), are extroverted, and win over people easily. They are often great flirts and salespersons. Because of this, they easily get dates and get into relationships.

Vulnerable narcissists are quite different, but like their grandiose cousins, they are highly self-centered. Vulnerable narcissists are often shy, needy, easily offended, and emotional. They aren't the types who will rise to the top and be in charge of an organization, but they will be "in charge" by passive-aggressively calling HR and complaining about someone they don't like.

They are always on the lookout for any little slip-up that offends them. They are the ones that tell you how much they love you, and how loving they are, and yet threaten to harm you or themselves when you don't tell them what they want to hear. They seem mild-mannered, but will call you every name in the book in private if you are their partner and don't give them attention. They are the types who will gossip about you anonymously or try to "cancel" you over something innocent you may have said years ago (3).

I think it is reasonable to say that those who are narcissists by my definition are indeed operating with many toxic assumptions and behaviors, and it's very possible the person you are addicted to is an actual narcissist, but it may also be the case that they don't rise to that level.

While I am reluctant to label someone a toxic person or narcissist (especially without knowing them), people, all people in fact, behave in toxic ways, but some way more than others.

Rather than thinking of a person as "toxic" I prefer to think more in terms of people exhibiting a range of toxic behaviors. Some people have worked on themselves and thus practice few of these behaviors, and when they do, the impact is minimal.

Others not only have a lot of these toxic behaviors, but the impact on others is huge.

For example, your partner may tell a small lie that they later come clean about, versus a partner who lies all the time, about big things, and never takes responsibility for any of them.

As a person's toxic behaviors increase in number and severity, it is increasingly fair to consider them "toxic." It's very possible your ex (or current partner) has a significant number of severely toxic behaviors.

As a hypnotist, I use what is called the "Meta Model" to get people to clearly define their own assumptions and motives and that of others.

This is important, because at the end of the day, calling someone "toxic" because you feel upset by them isn't useful in dealing with them or moving past them. Once you break down the problem into clear behaviors, then you can fully address the issues to move on and avoid people with these behaviors in the future.

So, what even makes behavior toxic? I propose that a behavior is toxic if it causes dysfunction emotionally, socially, and physically, to the person acting that way, and to others, which is similar to my definition of a narcissist.

This includes, of course, very serious things like any form of abuse, and cheating, but also communication strategies that break down relationships, like yelling, screaming, name-calling, or giving "the silent treatment."

Toxic communication and behaviors can be aggressive, passive, and passive-aggressive.

Aggressive behavior includes screaming, physical aggression, threats, getting in someone's face, calling them names or put-downs, and getting in sarcastic "digs."

Passive behavior includes things like "the silent treatment," not standing up for yourself or others when it's important, refusing to communicate when communication is necessary, and "checking out" of a relationship, including through coping mechanisms like using substances or playing video games all day. We often think of passive behavior as non-toxic, but it can be just as toxic and damaging as aggressive behavior.

Passive-aggressive behaviors combine both above behaviors, in that you are passive to the person's face, but behind the scenes, you are aggressive. This includes actions like constantly posting generally negative details about a relationship on social media designed to anger a partner, gossiping about a partner to others, taking revenge on them by neglecting household duties, or any petty, covert action designed to hurt them.

This chapter may seem very academic, but I want to be sure to define my terms.

Plus, as you move on in this book, you'll see that one thing that almost always happens when you are in a relationship with a toxic person, is that they draw you into their toxicity. Over time, people in toxic relationships often mirror the toxic behavior that they are trying to avoid.

I know many people who lament that their toxic partner yells, screams, and calls them names, yet that is how they engage others as well.

In fact, I have largely left the "toxic relationship" space on TikTok because of the toxicity of people calling out toxic relationships. The focus of some creators is not on healing or living a better life, and helping others do the same, but on things like revenge and obsession with their toxic exes.

Unfortunately, as your toxic relationship becomes more familiar to you, and you live in survival mode, you are more likely to mimic unhealthy behaviors rather than healthy ones. I'll address this more in chapter 14.

You may have noticed in the story of Mark it was difficult at times to tell who the toxic person was. Was it Steve? Was it Christy? Or even Mark for becoming obsessed with what Christy was doing? The answer is, "all of the above" at varying levels.

So, be careful whom you call toxic…because it might be you who gets called that next!

CHAPTER 6

Are You *Really* Addicted?

As I mentioned, you won't find partner or ex addiction in any DSM manual. You also can't go to your doctor to get medicine for it. This may change at some point, but as of now, if you feel like you're addicted to an ex, you may get funny looks if you tell people about it.

When I started to explore the behaviors that people have with exes, even toxic ones, I realized that it does meet the definition of an addiction in many ways.

The only real addictions I have experienced are food and coffee. I am not addicted to the former anymore, but happily remain coffee-addicted, enjoying a few cups a day. Everything else that is commonly addictive, I either have no desire to try, or else I consume in moderation.

But, I have definitely experienced addiction to partners, and the pain of going through a break-up with them, even if they were toxic. As I'll explain in more detail later, just because your partner leaves, or you decide to finally leave them, doesn't mean a large part of your brain is on board with that.

In one study, researchers recruited people who were still in love with their exes, and did brain scans of them. The study was fascinating in that their brains scans were very similar to the brain scans of people who were going through cocaine cravings and withdrawal (4).

For now, let's focus on the signs of addiction and how what you feel for your current toxic partner or ex absolutely fits with this definition. If you're a loved one or healer working with someone who is addicted, you will likely see these signs in that person.

I'm going to list the signs of addiction and how each relates to your relationship with someone toxic that you're romantically entangled with.

As you'll see, addiction isn't about enjoyment. It's an issue of not being able to stop doing something you're used to. A lot of people assume that drug addicts are sitting around partying all the time feeling great. But, if you know anybody who is addicted to anything, this is far from the truth.

Podcaster and professor Dr. Andrew Huberman defines addiction as "a progressive narrowing of the things that bring you pleasure." In other words, as you'll see, the more addicted you are, the more likely you are to do what you do because you want to *avoid feeling bad* rather than feeling a lot of good feelings.

So, let's get into the standard signs of addiction and how these apply to those who are stuck on someone toxic.

1. You can't stop even though you want to

This one is likely pretty obvious. How many times have you declared internally, or even to others, that you just need to leave your toxic partner? Or, declared you need to move on and stop thinking about them? Is it 100 times? 1000?

A client of mine, Sandy, did virtually everything she could to get over her toxic ex. Even though he cheated on her, and was seeing other women, she still went on dates with him occasionally, and even decided to live with him, knowing he was seeing other women.

She *knew* he was bad for her. She *declared* he was bad for her. She had tried things like willpower, blocking him, and other "conscious mind" solutions to the problem, and yet she still found herself going back to him. This may seem very familiar.

2. You continue in your addiction despite adverse consequences

Almost everyone I know addicted to a toxic person will relate to this. You continue reaching out to them, humoring them, covering for them, staying with them, and giving them "one more chance."

You do this knowing that you will continually not only be disappointed, but likely experience emotional, physical, and financial harm.

We think it's clearly addictive when a drug addict uses their drug despite the intense consequences, but many of us who have been addicted to toxic people have experienced similar levels of adverse consequences.

A toxic person provides many of the same adverse consequences that drugs do. Think about it: drugs abuse your body. They abuse your mind. They cause you to become a different person. They cause you to go broke. Toxic people provide the same exact consequences.

I know many people who were addicted to toxic partners who lost thousands of dollars covering for them, paying their bills, and more. One potential client (who sadly didn't show up for a follow-up appointment) was spending hundreds of dollars a week to pay the bills of an emotionally abusive "boyfriend" (who was still living with his actual girlfriend). Even though she was a single mother going broke, she continued this practice.

Yet, when presented with the prospect that working with me would literally save her hundreds a month after my fee, because she would quit sending money to him, she still convinced herself she didn't have money for my services or products. This is truly addictive behavior!

3. Tolerance: you allow more and more mistreatment

In terms of substance addiction, tolerance is when your body becomes more and more adapted to the substance, that it requires more of that substance to feel a "high."

This also happens with toxic people. You become very "used" to their bad behavior. Nothing even fazes you anymore. If someone you just met yelled, screamed, and talked to you the way your partner does (or ex did), you'd run far away from that person! But you tolerate and accept these behaviors from the toxic person in your life.

You tolerate cheating, lying, word games, substance abuse, your partner not contributing, verbal abuse, physical abuse, and all sorts of awful treatments you would never allow your friends, family, or kids to endure.

In fact, after a while, the mistreatment seems normal, and you believe that you deserve it.

4. Withdrawal: you become anxious when they're not around

In terms of substance abuse, withdrawal is when the lack of a substance makes you feel bad, antsy, and have cravings. This is ultimately what keeps people addicted, and is a result of dopamine dysregulation, which I'll get into more in a later chapter.

Addicts are rarely chasing a good time once they are addicted. They are just trying not to feel horrible from the feelings of withdrawal.

Anyone addicted to someone toxic knows all about this. You "need" to check up on their social media. You crave a text from them. You get lonely at midnight and if a text comes in, you feel relief. If they don't text you back quickly enough, you start to get edgy. You may even get sick to your stomach when you think of not being with them.

Withdrawal is ultimately what keeps you addicted to your partner.

5. Your day is centered around them (even if negative)

This one is obvious. A drug addict will literally spend their entire day thinking about drugs and working to get their drugs of choice. In the brain scan study I previously mentioned, some participants said they thought about their exes around 85% of their waking day!

If you're addicted to someone toxic, you may be doing the same thing. There are many ways your day can be centered around someone toxic. It may be that you think about them all day, or spend time with them, if you are still partnered up or casually seeing them.

In many cases, your day is centered around them in either a negative way, or a strange mix of love and hate.

Many people believe that they can't be addicted to someone if their feelings are primarily negative.

For example, when my clients explain to me why they talk about their ex all the time and stalk their social media, they will say that they don't do it because they love them, but rather, it's a drive that is rooted in hate. They believe this is a good thing and means they are "over" their ex…but not so fast.

There is brain scan research that shows that the neural pathways related to strong romantic love are nearly the same as the pathways for strong hate (5). What this means is that there truly is a fine line between addictive love and addictive hate.

The hard truth is that even if your day revolves around hating your ex or partner, you're still addicted.

For example, watching videos about toxic people…creating social media statuses about how awful your ex is…bringing your ex up whenever you meet with your friends…talking about them on dates to complain about them… These are all examples where your day is centered around this person. And, if you do these things a lot, you are likely still addicted.

6. You turn into a different person

When someone is addicted to a substance, they often change. The person who may have been happy, responsible, clean, and law-abiding, turns into the opposite of their former self.

This happens when you are with someone toxic for a long time.

Many clients I work with have come to me as a shell of their former selves. They used to be outgoing and love life. When they come to me, they are hesitant and bitter.

They used to be caring and trusting, but when I first see them, they are resentful and suspicious.

They used to take care of their bodies and minds, and now they neglect basic elements of their health. Many have gained significant weight or are dangerously underweight.

They were deeply religious and spiritual, but now they find themselves regularly doing unethical things they got into because of their partner, including constantly lying and covering up things.

This is what happens when you have spent so much time with a toxic person. You turn into them in some ways, and develop coping strategies that allow you to survive, like substance use or other bad habits.

7. You neglect your obligations and duties for them (work, school, parenting, etc.)

Finally, when you're addicted, you often neglect many things in your life.

Most of the clients I work with come to me having let so much of their life deteriorate. They have given up their dreams, hobbies, and friends, all because of the toxic person in their life.

Many have let their health slide, because their toxic partner didn't allow them to exercise or insisted on sabotaging their weight loss efforts.

Many people addicted to toxic people have neglected their relationships with their children, or put them in harm's way, so their own children barely want a relationship. Many of their children have mental health issues because of their parents' toxic relationship.

One client of mine is just now repairing her relationship with her daughter, because she chose to bring her toxic partner into her house after knowing him only for a few months, and let's just say he wasn't going to win any "parent of the year" awards. If we're honest, by her making that choice, she isn't going to win any awards either, but thankfully she is taking responsibility for her choices and healing.

Even if your toxic partner is now an "ex" you still likely neglect many duties for them. Think of how much time you spend checking up on them, dealing with them if they reach out, or even seeing them if you are still tempted to do that.

One client I worked with spent many nights driving outside her toxic ex's job to see if he had truly moved on or not, because she believed he was dating a co-worker. That time added up to hours a week. Those hours could have been used to do all sorts of positive and empowering things like working out, starting a business, or even pursuing her art hobby, which she loved.

Hopefully this chapter has opened your eyes, that you may truly be addicted to your toxic partner or ex. If you are a friend, family member, therapist, or coach, this insight will help you understand the person in your life you care about.

Now that you understand that it is something that is addictive in nature, let's talk about how you got addicted in the first place.

Chapter 7

You're Used To Being You

Every day, my client Rochelle woke up to her boyfriend passed out from staying up smoking weed and playing video games all night.

She would drag his body to the bed, and clean up all the trash around his computer, even as she was scrambling so she wouldn't be late for work.

Then, when he would finally wake up around noon, she'd send him angry texts from work, trying to get him to do a modicum of work around the house.

She'd get home, and nothing would be done, so she'd have to do most of the work herself.

Occasionally, he would get angry at her "nagging" and he would threaten her or put his hands on her.

If you have never been in a relationship like this, it may seem absurd to put up with this behavior, but when you're in a toxic relationship long enough, it becomes normal.

Obviously logically, this is never "normal." But, your unconscious mind isn't logical. Here is how you can eventually consider something like this normal, and it goes back to how your unconscious mind develops habits.

The unconscious mind learns "experientially" rather than "academically." For example, Rochelle knew logically that everything about her situation I mentioned above was not right, but her unconscious mind was learning that it was normal.

The way we learn experientially (developing unconscious habits) boils down to two things: emotions and repetition. They are often paired. This is how you have gotten stuck in unhealthy habits and also developed positive habits.

When I was in high school, I had some great teachers, but sadly I barely remember a lot of what they taught me. The same is likely true for you.

What *do* you remember from high school? You probably remember funny things that made you laugh, like pranks, unless the prank was on *you*, then you may remember it because it deeply embarrassed you. Similarly, if someone threatened you or some tragedy happened to you or another person, you likely remember that.

You remember your first love, dates, heartbreak, and other emotionally stimulating events. You likely remember some things from classes that you were genuinely interested in, but less from classes that weren't very relevant to you.

You may remember particularly mean or nice teachers, or ones who were unusually attractive or quirky.

Emotional experiences, particularly strong ones, are how we learn and make sense of the world. They are what get us to pay attention, both positively and negatively.

You may have learned that love is amazing from your first crush and you're still seeking that feeling again. Maybe you learned from your first rejection that love is cruel, people are mean, and you are now afraid to ask anyone out for fear of rejection.

Our brains are wired for this to happen because this helps us survive. Emotions give internal perceptive relevance to outside events. They tell us that an outside stimulus has a particular impact, and our brains then generalize the emotional experience out to future potential events.

For example, a child who touches a hot stove learns to never do that again. There is no need for repetition.

Many traumas are developed this way. A dog bites us and we learn (unconsciously) that dogs are scary, so we then become scared of dogs.

These now become your "normal." You don't touch stoves and don't go around dogs.

The problem is that in some cases, what we have learned through emotion isn't in alignment with our goals or even logical reality.

In terms of partner addiction, you may have learned that if you don't pick up after your partner, you'll get screamed at. Or they'll whine for an hour. Or, it won't get done, which makes you feel upset. Instead of feeling upset for long, you learned to just to pick up after them.

Whenever you try to get them to communicate about the relationship, they get angry and filled with rage. Since that scares you, you just avoid it all together, and end up caring less about improving the relationship and just put your head down and exist as best as possible.

You also likely have internalized many beliefs about yourself from the emotions your toxic partner has generated.

Every time you feel sad, dejected, or worthless, your unconscious mind is learning that these feelings accurately represent reality. You go from being happy, trusting, and feeling like you can handle life, to feeling sad, insecure, and like you are a victim of circumstances.

And, as I'll explain further later, if you are in a cycle of trauma and trauma responses, you are learning how to stay in these survival responses and emotions.

In addition to learning through emotions, we also learn experientially through repetition. The more often we do something, the more likely we are to do it again. This is worth repeating (see what I'm doing here?).

The more often we do something, the more likely we are to do it again.

I always say that the reason you do what you do most of the time isn't because you had a "bad childhood" or whatever it is you attribute it to. The reason you do what you do is because you did it the day before. And the day before that. And before that. Of course, it may have started because of your bad childhood, but you do it today because you did it yesterday.

The main reason Rochelle acted the way she did toward her boyfriend was because she did it so often, it was now normal. And, unfortunately, the more she did it, the more it became even more normal, to the point that after the break-up she even missed it a little bit.

Of course, this makes no logical sense, but the unconscious mind isn't logical, but rather experiential!

When you pair emotion with repetition, you have a recipe to create a strong habit or addiction.

Emotion and repetition are how strong habits are formed. The longer Rochelle cared for her boyfriend like a mother, the more she felt all kinds of feelings (including fear if she didn't do it for him), and the more she continued repeating the habit.

Over time, this experiential learning created a new "normal" for her. Even though academically she knew it wasn't good for her, and hardly normal, her unconscious mind considered it normal.

The human brain tries to maintain familiarity at all costs. The brain tends to conflate familiarity with safety. This is why people will struggle to give up familiar, but unhealthy behaviors, like overeating, gambling, mistreating their bodies in some way, or staying with a toxic partner who is bad for them.

All the experiences you have had are physically wired into your brain as connections between neurons. Neurons form the basis of your thoughts and memories. Neurons form connections with one another, and this is where our experiences get wired into our brain.

The more often we have felt a certain way, or thought a certain way, the stronger the connections between neurons become, as they get reinforced over and over. Imagine a little wire between neurons where electrical activity flows. Every time you re-experience something, that wire gets thicker and thicker. Once this connection is firmly established, your brain will maintain it and it will become automatic and this is your "normal" and "autopilot."

The brain will resist creating a new connection when the old ones are so strong. So, your brain is literally physically wired to be familiar with your toxic ex or partner, even if they aren't good for you.

Rochelle's toxic situation was so familiar that leaving it was scary to her unconscious mind, in part because it was firmly wired into her brain.

Even after she made the safe and healthy choice to leave, she still felt a pull back to the familiar. Fortunately, we worked through that using hypnosis and accountability.

The good news is that the more you make changes and establish new thoughts, feelings, and actions, you create new brain wiring and extinguish the old wiring. This is because the brain is *neuroplastic*, meaning that it can rewire and create new neural connections. This is great news and I'll explain it in more depth later.

Chapter 8

Your Three Brains

A client, Charles, once told me that he felt like his brain was "on fire" as he struggled to get over a toxic ex. He noticed that he could go from deeply hating his ex to wanting her back within literal seconds.

As he saw her with her new boyfriend (whom she met while she was with him), he felt feelings of absolute rage. Yet moments later he was nearly in tears, missing her, ready to take her back.

In chapter one, I told a story that illustrates how our conscious and unconscious minds often have different impulses and goals. Since then, I've written a lot about the conscious mind and the unconscious mind. These aren't brain structures. These are just conceptual divisions of the mind.

In this chapter, I'm going to write about the different parts of our brains which are essentially at war with one another, which will help you understand the conflicting desires you have.

As I move on to explain what happens when you're addicted to someone (and how to overcome it), this section will be a very important reference point, because it will help you begin to understand why you do and feel what you do. You may feel like all this brain stuff is pointless and you might as well skip over it. I hope you resist this urge, because this is very important.

So, the brain isn't so much one structure as it is a combination of structures. Some of these structures are older in terms of our evolutionary history. We share these structures with all sorts of other animals.

We laugh when a dog tries to get um…frisky…with someone's leg, or when we learn that male turkeys will try to mate with plastic female turkeys (or anything similar). Surely, they are smart enough to know that legs and plastic turkeys aren't "the real thing," right??

Yet, how is this really any different from someone looking at pornography or relying on a plastic device for pleasure?

We laugh at two cats who should know better that are hissing at each other and growling, but we often think it's acceptable for two human strangers to "hiss and growl" by calling each other names on social media for hours.

If you were to look at what most of us pay attention to, in terms of our basic desires, habits, and instincts, we often, in our unconscious behaviors at least, act more like other animals than we act uniquely human.

Why is this the case?

The "triune brain" concept was developed by neuroscientist Paul MacLean in the 1960s. While recent developments suggest his ideas are too neat and tidy for what is happening, since the brain is more adaptive than he proposed, I'm going to use the "triune brain" model here because it is useful. Just know that in the field of neuroscience, things are always changing as we learn more about the brain. This chapter is *not* an endorsement of this model, but it is very useful.

MacLean divided the brain into three regions, the reptilian brain, the limbic brain, and the neocortex. One can even make the case that the "brain" extends out beyond the actual brain, as there are neurons in the heart and gut as well, to the point that some researchers call each of these areas "the second brain." So, when I speak of the reptilian and limbic brains, just be aware that these areas may include neurons in the heart and gut.

These structures are of various ages in terms of human evolution, and often don't work together very well.

The human brain is less of a new, "out of the box" powerful computer and more of a computer that is cobbled together of various generational parts, and running software that is haphazardly upgraded and patched.

For you video game nerds, our brain is like an Atari 2600 that keeps getting newer parts added to it, and software patches, rather than being like a brand new PS5 (or whatever a brand new system is as you're reading this) fresh out of the box.

The "reptilian brain" is focused on survival, and consists of the brain stem and cerebellum. The brain stem regulates heartbeat, breathing, and other vital organ functions.

The reptilian brain is a part of where the fight, flight, or freeze response happens, which is why lower animals with very undeveloped brains will respond in these ways.

The "limbic system" or paleomammalian complex, consists of the subcortical regions, and this includes structures involved in emotion, feelings, desire, motivation, and rewards. This is also where many components of the fight, flight, and freeze response occur.

The limbic system is very important to understanding addiction to a toxic person, because this is where emotions, rewards, and trauma responses are largely located.

You can thank your limbic system for why you may likely be motivated to eat sugary foods and scroll mindlessly, and feel unmotivated to get to the gym and consume healthier food.

You can also thank your limbic system for feeling a strong desire for someone who is attractive, but toxic, and unstimulated by someone who is kind and nice, but unattractive.

Your limbic system, which as I mentioned includes neurons outside of the brain, is also why you get stomach aches when you're stressed, but also butterflies in that same area when you fall in love. It's why your heart can literally ache after a breakup.

As I type this, my cat Coconut is on my lap sleeping. If he heard a loud noise, his reptilian brain and limbic system would be active as he assessed a potential threat. If he felt threatened, he might freeze, run, or start clawing my legs.

If someone downstairs happened to shake the bag of cat food, he'd immediately wake up and scurry downstairs hoping for food, meowing and rubbing up against anyone who was near the food (unless he perceived them as a threat).

If he were not neutered, and a female cat was in heat nearby, he might be "thinking" about something else, or more accurately, "feeling" something else, since his limbic system would be driving him to turn into a kitty player.

Because he doesn't have an advanced neo-mammalian brain or neocortex like humans have, he is always going to act like this, unless for some reason his limbic system was feeling some other strong emotion (like if he were sick, very tired, or scared).

This is why he would be siring kittens if he weren't neutered. He only goes by what feels rewarding, or what doesn't.

The reason he *isn't* siring kittens is because someone with an advanced neocortex (me!) knew that if he were to sire kittens, that wouldn't be a good idea. So, I used my advanced brain to deliberate about it, plan ahead, and logically get him neutered.

But, as smart as Coconut is for a cat, we have no evidence that he is capable of deliberating in this way himself.

And, fortunately, many humans before me used their neocortices to take the time to deliberate, plan, and work out how to neuter a cat safely for a decent price.

Our highly-developed neo-mammalian brains are why we have the advanced technologies that we do. A part of the neocortex is the frontal lobe, and humans have a particularly developed frontal lobe.

The frontal lobe allows us to plan, deliberate, imagine the future, and explore possibilities. It's where things like logical deliberation and speech are located. It is also the seat of emotional regulation and delaying gratification.

However, this doesn't mean we are like the Star Trek character Mr. Spock. We are creatures with reptilian and limbic structures too, and these parts are all connected.

For example, I didn't just neutrally (no pun intended!) determine Coconut needed neutered. I was motivated emotionally: I didn't want to have to deal with a bunch of kittens running around. I also felt good knowing that his health was being prioritized. And, I always feel good when I make a decision I know is morally right and responsible (keeping the cat population controlled).

As you can see, we are mostly guided by our reptilian and limbic brains. Emotion is how we are motivated. If we aren't motivated, we aren't going to do anything.

Even something that you think is mundane, like going to work, is really filled with all kinds of emotional motivations. You go to that job because you likely enjoy the money, or fear what would happen if you quit (like, for example, you would lose your house, or your boss would get mad).

The reptilian and limbic brains operate underneath conscious awareness to a large degree. We don't often know why we do what do, or feel what we feel. And these feelings and motivations are often strong, illogical, and we act on them and explain them logically later.

Usually even when we make a "logical" decision, it's highly emotional in nature, and we end up doing what we would have done anyway.

For example, you may have been great at "logically" defending why you were with a toxic partner to your family and friends, by saying things like "nobody understands them like I do!" or "they had a bad childhood."

In reality, you were with them for limbic brain reasons, and any "logic" was just explaining your emotional decision to the best of your ability.

In my hypnosis and coaching practice, my goal for client growth isn't to somehow "transcend" our different brain structures, but rather to integrate them, allowing them to get along as well as possible.

The first step to this is understanding what is going on inside your brain. Throughout the rest of this book, I'll be writing about the brain in a way that assumes that our brain contains structures that often compete for our attention.

Chapter 9

Short-Term Infatuation's Brain Drain

There is a good reason that so many poems, songs, and other forms of art are related to love in some way. When humans fall in love, our brains change significantly, and we don't even know it. I'm going to write about some of these changes, and explain how these changes have bonded you to your toxic partner. This is going to be a longer chapter, but a very important one.

When I was in high school, a good friend of mine fell in love for the first time. And, it broke his brain. While I was used to seeing him regularly, he disappeared off the face of the earth socially. He spent every free moment with his new girlfriend. And, he started drinking excessively and behaving recklessly, by imitating the behavior of her and her friends. It all culminated in him drinking so much he ended up driving while intoxicated. He pulled over and puked in someone's driveway while being blackout drunk.

Even to this day, he describes what happened to him almost like being under a curse or spell.

There is a reason I introduced the triune brain before starting this chapter, because what is happening in this chapter is mostly a limbic brain phenomenon. And, if you recall from the last chapter, the limbic brain is about rewards, emotions, and motivations, and is largely outside our logical and conscious awareness.

We evolved to fall in love and pair bond with a partner. While this process may feel magical and spiritual, there is a very good, logical reason we do this: to reproduce, and stick around in a relationship long enough to raise a child. Humans never would have survived if we didn't have these two very strong innate desires. And, our brains and bodies change significantly to ensure all of this will happen.

In this chapter, I'm going to address what happens to your brain when you fall in love and become infatuated with someone initially. In the next chapter, I'll cover longer-term bonding (necessary for child rearing) and what that does to your brain to keep you stuck on someone toxic.

So, as you go through the falling in love and partnering processes, your brain is changing in very significant ways that are designed to keep you singularly emotionally focused on your partner.

You may think that nature isn't very smart because you ended up falling in love and bonding with a complete jerk who isn't good for you or your kids.

But remember…falling in love happens in your limbic brain so it isn't logical. While there is debate scientifically about why we fall for particular people, it includes factors like someone's immunity, their health, and their evolutionary fitness.

I'm going to explain the process, based on research, for heterosexual relationships. The research on lesbian, gay, and bisexual brain chemistry, attraction, and bonding isn't as developed. This also applies to other sexual orientations. However, much of what I'm going to present in the next few chapters will likely still be helpful even if you aren't heterosexual, but please keep my caveat in mind.

Men and women tend to have different things that they find attractive in a partner. Things like height, age, build, and personality factors all play a role. For example, most women prefer a guy who is taller and at least slightly older than they are. They also tend to prefer men who are charismatic and have power and status in some form.

At the end of the day, women seem to look for men who have traits, both in appearance and personality, which show they are good providers and protectors.

Men overall seem to look for traits that signal fertility (like longer, thicker hair, body shape, and youth).

There are obviously variations, and what I am writing is the case generally, which means there are outliers and overall, people have different preferences.

Keep in mind this is all happening unconsciously. You may protest that your toxic ex didn't protect you or provide for you at all!

Your unconscious mind isn't logical. It thinks kind of like this: "tall and burley = can provide for you" or "he's a rebel who doesn't care what others think = he can protect you."

I know I will surely offend someone in this chapter. Keep in mind that I'm not saying any of these make sense or are morally right. In fact, I work with my hypnosis clients to become aware of these factors, so they can choose potential dates based on more logical, conscious factors like their values, rather than being driven mainly by unconscious factors, like someone's height, body shape, or charisma.

I've gotten into some of the reasons your brain changes based on attraction, and now let's get into possible brain chemistry changes that happen when you fall for someone. As with anything in the field of neuroscience, what I'm about to explain could easily change and is based on certain current theories and research.

Dopamine

The first thing when you fall in love is that your brain's motivation and reward system goes into overdrive. And, it involves dopamine.

The actual role of the dopamine system is misunderstood in popular culture. It is often thought of as the "pleasure chemical" but dopamine is best thought of as more of a motivation chemical.

The pleasure comes from having finally achieved the thing you are motivated to get, and even the anticipation of that event. This involves dopamine, but also the brain's opioid system (which includes endorphins).

Dopamine is the reason humans survived throughout our history. If you are hungry, it is the dopamine system that is causing you to go out and find food. It is dopamine that makes the process of hunting rewarding, and why that first taste of food tastes great, but each subsequent bite doesn't taste as good.

As we have gotten more and more of the thing we want, dopamine levels normalize, and we don't feel as good as we did initially, and may even start to feel bad.

When you are "in love" your dopamine circuits are lighting up, and you are highly motivated to see that person, and when you, do it feels amazing. I'm talking "the world is brighter and songs sound better" amazing. Do you remember that feeling? It truly is a great feeling, and has inspired many works of art throughout human history.

But, remember dopamine is about motivation. When you *aren't* getting what you are finding pleasurable, and your dopamine levels are low, you become highly motivated to get back the happiness that you once felt.

This process of dopamine levels dropping is called withdrawal. Your brain wants dopamine levels to get back to baseline, and the only thing that will satisfy this is getting the thing you now crave.

This is why a starving human will be highly motivated to find food, or a cocaine addict will do anything to get cocaine. You may have wondered why drug addicts who are otherwise law-abiding will lie, steal, and cheat to get their drug. Well, now you know!

It's also why if you're in love with someone, and they don't text you for an hour, you may become jittery, upset, and suspicious. You may spend that time meticulously checking their social media to see if they were active or liked another photo. It is the dopamine system that is motivating you to do this. And, as you'll see in a moment, another chemical, norepinephrine, is making you super focused and intense about it.

When they finally text you, you feel better, and wonder why in the world you spent the previous two hours acting that way.

But the dopamine system doesn't just want you to get back to baseline...it changes what baseline even is! When you feel a dopamine "high" often enough, your dopamine receptors can become less sensitive to dopamine (called "downregulation"), which means you need more dopamine in the future to get the same good feeling you had previously.

So, while holding someone's hand and seeing them for an hour were all you needed to feel good at first, you need to spend more and more time with them, and escalate romantically, to feel the same pleasure in the future.

During the "infatuation" phase, most people who are in love are experiencing this boost of dopamine. It's not odd to be going through this. However, keep in mind that just as the human brain craves high sugar foods that are bad for us in excess, your brain's dopamine reward system really doesn't care about being moral and ethical.

So, it is very common to be getting a dopamine-inflated boost from someone who is attractive at an emotional, limbic level (i.e. they are physically attractive or charming), but who isn't necessarily a well-rounded, adjusted person. This explains a lot, doesn't it?

Norepinephrine

When I was getting a root canal, the endodontist was numbing my tooth, and after he injected something into me, I felt a rush of intense feelings that bordered on anxiety. I asked, "what was in that?!!"

He explained that it was epinephrine, which got us talking about body and brain chemistry. I think he was a little surprised we were discussing this, but in his mind, I'm sure it beat small talk about the weather.

Norepinephrine is a form of adrenaline (it is also called noradrenaline) and it seems to ramp up when we're in love.

Norepinephrine is a powerful chemical that allows us to feel exceptionally alert and focused, and even stressed. And, it makes us feel highly focused so we can direct our attention on a task that is emotionally important to us.

Think back to the scenario I mentioned earlier, where maybe your partner didn't text you back for a few hours, and you started to get suspicious.

It was norepinephrine that helped your brain stay keenly focused on checking up on them on social media. Imagine if you were motivated to be that meticulous at other tasks, like exercising or starting your business!

Norepinephrine is why when you're infatuated with someone, you feel strongly focused on them and have a lot of energy to see them.

Along with dopamine, it's why you make sure you see them for hours a day, want to live with them right away, and may even literally be texting them for hours a day. It may be why you often feel "manic" in your desire to see them.

It's also why you can stay up until 3:00 AM talking with them, and get up the next day feeling just fine.

Of course, the downside of this extreme focus is that when you're giving this other person your attention, you're also neglecting other duties, tasks, and friends.

Another downside is that norepinephrine is ultimately a stress hormone that is part of the fight, flight, or freeze response. So it isn't necessarily healthy to have consistently elevated norepinephrine levels.

I remember my first experience with norepinephrine (and dopamine and all the other chemicals we are talking about). After meeting a particular girl at a junior high dance one night, my limbic brain was smitten. I remember that I couldn't sleep that night. I was so "hopped up" and excited that my mind swirled all night long.

It turns out she wasn't exactly smitten back, but my brain didn't care. Eventually I remember feeling that way about another girl, who likely also wasn't smitten back (junior high was a tough period).

As with dopamine, norepinephrine isn't a "moral" chemical, and what it leads us to focus on may not exactly be good for us in the long term.

Many people have placed their focus on toxic people, and neglected family, friends, and even put their dreams on hold.

Your limbic brain is going to make you feel like "love can conquer all," even if logically there is no way this person will ever be a healthy partner in a healthy relationship.

Now is a good time to bring this up: when your brain is in this infatuation stage, you are perceptually less likely to notice red flags, if you notice them at all.

That's right, brain scan research shows that the parts of the brain responsible for critically assessing someone socially become impaired when you're infatuated, at least when you're engaging the object of your infatuation (6). So, what happens when the organ responsible for perceiving red flags becomes unable to perceive? Well…you make bad decisions.

This explains why when you're in love he is an artistic type whom nobody understands. And, all of his exes, debt-collectors, and the justice system are clearly out to get him based on giant misunderstandings, and he just happens to be between jobs and needs a place to stay.

After your brain gains some composure, you realize he was just a chronically out-of-work house painter with a criminal record who was using you for a place to stay and sex, and who played other women the same way… and come to think of it, you're not even sure if he ever actually painted a house because he didn't know what primer was when you brought it up.

When you're in love, he's a shaman and an innovative businessman. Later you realize he was just a drug dealer who was high all the time.

When you're in a state of infatuation, she's "a little high-maintenance at times" and "goes slightly overboard when having fun." When you come to your senses, you understand that she flirted with anyone with a pulse (even in front of you), drained your savings account to finance her shopping addiction, and abused alcohol.

Your friends saw this right away, but their brains weren't altered chemically like yours was.

What this means is that when you are falling in love, your brain is changing a lot, and you're likely not even aware it is changing. So, while you're making bad decisions, squeezing out friends, neglecting regular tasks that keep you mentally and physically healthy (one study found the average person gains 17 pounds in the first year of a relationship), you explain it away as if it's perfectly natural (7).

Does this sound maybe like when you're infatuated, you're on drugs? Well, it is kind of like that.

Prairie voles are cute little rodents that are similar to humans in that they tend to pair up romantically with one another. This makes them a subject of a lot of research, including where some of the research in this book comes from.

In one study, they gave "in love" prairie voles drugs, and they found something rather interesting: the prairie voles couldn't get high. So, the researchers concluded that the reason they couldn't get high on drugs was because they already were high...on love (8)!

The brain chemistry described in this chapter lasts anywhere from one to five years, depending on various factors. It's possible to feel this way after many years, or lose this feeling rather quickly.

Even if you don't feel it directly anymore, many people still "chase" that feeling in a toxic partner.

Also, I should note that it is very difficult to do precise research on the brain, because it would involve being a little too invasive. So, much of what I'm writing about on brain chemistry is speculative and based on emerging research. Ultimately brain chemistry can't be boiled down to two chemicals, and other chemical systems are involved in short-term bonding, including serotonin, and the brain's opioid and cannabinoid systems.

I have intentionally not discussed serotonin in depth, and I want to explain why. Different sources suggest different things about serotonin. While some sources suggest serotonin levels rise when you're infatuated, another study found something very fascinating, which is that serotonin transport is significantly disrupted, to an extent of that seen in Obsessive-Compulsive Disorder.

It found that "subjects who were in the early romantic phase of a love relationship were not different from OCD patients in terms of the density of the platelet 5-HT transporter" (9). In other words, it may explain why when you're in love, you're obsessed with your partner.

Okay, that's the short-term impact of love, so let's move onto longer-term bonding.

CHAPTER 10

YOUR BRAIN IS IN IT FOR THE LONG HAUL

Like I mentioned previously, your brain changes to get you very excited and motivated initially when you are into someone. Your brain knows that if you don't stay singularly focused on the object of your affection, humanity won't survive.

It also knows that the best way for a child to survive is if you stay bonded to your partner. Human children are particularly vulnerable, and unable to survive on their own for a significant timespan compared to other animals. Pair bonding ensured a better chance of childhood survival.

Remember, none of this is logical, so it has nothing to do with whether you logically want kids, can have kids, or have kids. This bonding may also happen regardless of sexual orientation.

So, when you pair up, your brain also releases chemicals that bond you to your partner long-term. Nature is wise in a very basic sense, but not so wise when it comes to picking a partner for the actual bond.

Let's talk about these mechanisms and why they can keep you addicted to someone.

Overdosin' on Oxytocin

One major chemical driver of bonding is oxytocin. Emerging research shows that this is particularly true in women. In fact, some women's brains seem to be more sensitive to oxytocin than others.

Oxytocin is known as the "cuddle chemical," and is called this because it gets released when people cuddle. It also gets released in abundance when you hold hands, make out, kiss, or have sexual relations with someone.

Oxytocin seems to facilitate social bonding in humans (and other animals). When it is released in your brain, it creates an emotional bond that is designed to last. As an example, oxytocin gets released when a mother gives birth, and it is oxytocin that bonds a mother to her children.

In one study with rats, when researchers blocked oxytocin in the brains of mother rats, they rejected their own offspring (10).

This shows you how important and powerful oxytocin is for

bonding.

This powerful chemical gets released when you get intimate with someone. Many women I know have tried to have "hook ups" and "one night stands" and found themselves strangely "catching feelings" for that person, despite not wanting to.

They went in thinking intimacy was emotionally neutral, but found out quickly that it isn't.

In the same way that infatuation changes your brain in ways you aren't aware of, the same is true of oxytocin.

Since we share these chemicals with animals, this process isn't logical and conscious, but rather emotional and largely unconscious.

So, if you have bonded through oxytocin with your partner, leaving them could be a real challenge. Think of your kids if you have them: what would it take for you to leave your kids? This may be how hard it feels to leave your partner.

Oxytocin may also explain why many women essentially become mothers to their toxic partners. Oxytocin encourages this type of bond. Many of my female clients treated their partners like children: cleaning up after them, making excuses for them, or even working multiple jobs so their partner could sit around all day and play video games.

Once you understand that your brain has bonded with your

partner through oxytocin, this all makes sense. It also now makes sense as to why it becomes difficult to leave.

I should note that oxytocin is often thought to be an empathy chemical, but that isn't entirely true. Oxytocin is more of a "tribal" chemical in that it promotes bonding with people within your "in group" but at the expense of those outside your group (11). So, this could explain a lot of the jealousy that can happen in relationships.

Keep Vasopressin On

I'm sure you're sick of these puns by now, but let's talk about vasopressin, another chemical that seems to be involved in long-term bonding and seems to be particularly relevant in men.

While men do bond through oxytocin, at least it seems so, they seem to bond through vasopressin significantly as well.

Vasopressin is a chemical of territoriality, territorial aggression, and marking territory. This explains why men tend to bond the way they do.

One day I was lifting weights on a machine at the gym next to a woman. Her boyfriend was standing beside her on the other side of her machine. Almost instinctively, when I sat down, he suddenly switched sides and positioned himself between my machine and hers. He then put his arm around her. There was no real logical reason to do this, except to perhaps guard his "territory."

This also explains why when men get jealous, they tend to do so in a way that is very territorial, even physically so. This may explain why guys get in physical altercations over their partners as well.

While oxytocin may lead to feelings of mothering, vasopressin may produce different results in terms of how it is expressed.

In terms of addiction, if you are a guy who bonded through vasopressin, you may feel weird feelings of protection and territoriality toward your partner, even if it isn't logical. You may even feel like protecting her "from herself." You may also find yourself getting insanely jealous related to her, and her interactions with other men. You may even get into physical fights over her, even if she was responsible for making the first move with the guy you're angry at.

Hormone Leveling

Finally, another way long-term bonding happens is through hormone equalization, at least in heterosexual relationships. Some research suggests that when men and women are paired up, men's testosterone levels decrease and women's levels increase (along with similar changes in estrogen) (6).

This has the effect of producing loyalty and increased similarity. It does this by reducing male risk taking and sexual desire, thus reducing the chances he'll cheat (as I'll discuss later, testosterone seems to interfere with oxytocin bonding), but it also makes both partners more alike.

This change ensures fidelity, and facilitates staying together long enough to raise a young child. Interestingly, becoming a father also reduces male testosterone levels, at least for a few years.

As you can see from this chapter and the last, nature really messes with our brains to ensure that humanity survives.

This also explains why you may have noticed that once someone is coupled up, they don't seem like the same person as before. They not only become more like their partner, but they focus mainly on hanging out and spending a lot of time together, and often give up many of their former pursuits and interests.

I didn't write these chapters to freak you out, or take away the magic of love and bonding, but rather to enlighten you about what is happening in your brain that you may not even be aware of. Once you understand what is happening, you can then start to address many of these changes.

I'll write more about this later when I offer solutions to modulating these chemical changes in chapters 19 and 20.

But now, let's discuss how toxic relationships specifically are addicting.

Chapter 11

Trauma Bonding Part 1: Intermittent Rewards and Punishments

Trauma bonding is the term for when someone who is mistreated or abused bonds with the person who is mistreating them. It is largely the result of the unpredictable (intermittent) behavior of the toxic person, who can elicit powerfully positive, but also powerfully negative, emotions from their victims.

This emotionally charged and unpredictable cycle of rewards and punishments keeps people stuck in toxic relationships and addicted to toxic people. In this chapter, I'm going to lay out how these rewards and punishments are the perfect recipe to keep you stuck on someone toxic.

One day my phone updated and there was a new app that

appeared on my screen. It was a block-based game like Tetris, but not quite the same. I thought about giving it a try just to see if it was Tetris.

I started playing it and it was fun. As I played, my high score went up, and I eventually wanted an even higher score.

There was some skill involved, but a lot of success, like Tetris, was based on which pieces the game gave me to work with. Some massive pieces were very difficult to work with and made the game challenging.

I found myself playing it more and more (and more and more), and caring about the high score more and more. The game even encouraged me by teasing my next score "milestone."

After a while, I found myself playing it not for fun as I did originally, but just to get a higher score. This led to me being both insanely frustrated, and also wanting to play it whenever I had a chance. I found it creeping into the time when I would normally read or do other healthy activities.

The game is designed to be addicting. It provides what psychologists call "intermittent rewards." This creates intermittent reinforcement, which is defined as an unpredictable system of providing a reward.

In plain English, this just means that the game does provide a reward, but it is neither consistent, nor guaranteed, nor completely tied to one's effort. The reward may come today, maybe tomorrow, or maybe next week (or in a year).

When the reward is significant enough to you (i.e. you really want it, and this includes rewards like love, affection, intimacy, and sex), intermittent rewards are very addictive.

Let me explain a classic study related to this. Researchers tested different ways of rewarding rats with food. They devised a system where rats could pull levers to get food.

Rats are smart enough to learn that pulling the lever delivers food. When food rewards were given based on a set number of lever pulls, rats would eat when they wanted food. So, if they learned that three pulls got them a morsel of food, they would pull it three times, or however many times they needed to get full. Then they would stop.

Researchers decided to test what rats would do if the lever and food connection was totally unpredictable, i.e. the rats could pull the lever once and get food one time, and the next time it may take 100 pulls, and so forth.

What they found is that these rats became obsessed with lever pulling. They would pull the lever all the time. They even stopped grooming and caring for themselves in other ways to focus on lever pulling (12).

Intermittent reinforcement leads to addictive behaviors,

because the reward is detached from the process to get the rewards. This confuses our limbic systems which believe "pulling the lever = food." But the problem is there is no consistency, so the limbic brain just "pulls the lever" all the time.

This is exactly how slot machines (and toxic relationships) work.

As soon as you walk into the casino, you see the potential rewards that a slot machine can give you flashing on the screen, including how much others have recently won. This is already priming you to want a large reward.

Once you start playing, you get small rewards that show you that winning is possible, and our brains enjoy that feeling. Now, the brain is working hard to restore that feeling. So, you keep playing through losses, because you win occasionally, and that big payout seems "just around the corner."

And, in a few hours, you do get a bigger payout. Now, you're convinced that you can get that bigger payout again, but also that you can get the even bigger payout advertised on the machine.

So, you keep playing, chasing, at minimum, the previous level of reward (to recap your investment) and hoping for a bigger one.

When I first got a 500-point high score in the block game, I was happy. But after that, it wasn't good enough, as I was teased the 1000-point score. But the problem, as I mentioned, is that this "work" of playing the game isn't directly connected to the actual outcome, even though a part of our brains thinks it is. Ultimately, the result is random and out of our control.

This is why when gambling, the house always wins. Sure, you can have better strategies, and use logic to control what you can, but in the end, there is just too much randomness, so you get addicted.

In unhealthy relationships, here is how intermittent rewards (and punishments) are established.

At first, everything is great with your partner, or at least you're *perceiving* that it's all great (remember, your brain is "high"). You're getting a lot of rewards. You are feeling great.

However, if your partner isn't emotionally healthy, or has communication issues, they will inevitably have moments of coldness and emotional distance. They happen at random, or at moments when you don't expect it. When they are like that, you miss the feeling of affection and love.

So, you "work" to get that feeling back. You try to please them, cover for them, or earn their love (like a rat pulling a lever). But it really doesn't work that well. It doesn't work because the problem is the internal reality of your partner; your behavior has nothing to do with it.

As time passes, these periods of coldness and distance grow and grow, and the periods of affection and passion decline. This makes your brain want those "payouts" even more. So, you chase them harder than ever.

And, you get payouts occasionally. Casinos know that they must pay out enough to keep you hooked. Nobody would gamble if they never paid out.

Unhealthy partners also pay out sometimes, and can be loving, affectionate, and intimate at moments. However, this is on their terms and therefore it is largely random, so it is disconnected from anything you're doing.

I hope that you can see how over time this is going to get you addicted. The more distant your partner is, and the more you crave something from them, the harder you work. Without a reward coming, you work harder and harder. Then you get a random reward, and your limbic brain thinks "ahhhh, that extra work must have done the trick!"

But then it doesn't succeed the next time, so you work even harder.

You might wonder why you do this if it doesn't make sense. Remember, your limbic brain isn't logical: it's emotional, and is based on survival, reward, and motivation.

Why do you eat sugary foods even though you want to lose weight?

Why do you scroll for hours on social media rather than get

work done?

Why do you drink a liquid all day that is made from a bean, and get angry and irritable if you don't get it (that's coffee by the way)?

Why do you inhale smoke from a stick and if you run out of these sticks, you'll leave your house at midnight and drive miles just to get one?

And, why do you still have feelings for someone who is bad for you? Why do you even find other people unattractive that you know are good for you because you're so stuck on this toxic person?

Sadly, we are just like those poor rats pulling levers for food and ignoring other aspects of life because of that.

So far, I have mainly written about intermittent rewards, but when you add intermittent punishments to the mix, it becomes even harder to leave.

Intermittent punishments are just as random as intermittent rewards, but this is when your partner causes you to feel more "negative" emotions like fear.

Intermittent punishments are also a nefarious way to get you addicted. But rather than chasing a random reward, you are avoiding being randomly punished. Intermittent punishments keep you constantly on edge and afraid.

Examples of intermittent punishments include: the silent

treatment, yelling, screaming, abuse, threatening to harm themselves, threatening to harm you, threatening to harm others, guilt-tripping you, taking away privileges, destroying things that are meaningful to you, and many other tactics.

Toxic people often use these intermittent punishments in part because they are volatile people. You never know when they will be in a good mood or bad mood. So, they may "fly off the handle" for something little and random.

You may come home from work in a good mood and have to worry that they will be "off" the entire evening. Even worse, you may have to worry that you will say something harmless, something that you have said hundreds of times before, and they will take it the wrong way and become verbally or physically abusive.

The typical reaction to intermittent punishments is to withhold any behavior that could lead to a potentially negative reaction. So, you "walk on eggshells" for fear of setting off your unpredictable partner. You may withhold doing positive things in your life because they might irritate your partner.

This keeps you addicted to them because you not only start to accept this pattern as your new "normal," but you fear their retribution if you decide to set boundaries, stand up for yourself, or cut them out of your life.

The most effective way to control someone is to provide both intermittent rewards and punishments. Toxic educational environments, religions (especially cults), and workplaces often utilize these tools to control others, whether intentionally or unintentionally.

This is one major way your toxic partner got you addicted to them. You simultaneously crave the good things you miss, like intimacy, passion, and charming words, while living in fear of their retribution.

This can cause you to develop a trauma response and become reactive, which I'll write about in the next few chapters.

Chapter 12

Trauma Bonding Part 2: What Is Trauma?

When you experience something that makes you feel unsafe, your unconscious mind (in this case your reptilian and limbic brains) works to protect you. It protects you in the same ways that it protects other animals: causing you to go into a fight, flight, or freeze response.

In animals, this is usually obvious. A rabbit, for example, will freeze to avoid being noticed by a predator. A wolf may fight back against a bear. And, a cheetah will sprint away from a threat.

We humans use all these responses as well, to varying degrees. If you were abused physically growing up, you may have learned that "disappearing" was the best way to avoid trouble, so you never spoke up and instead blended into the background of your family, which is essentially a type of freeze or flight response.

Maybe you dealt with an emotionally abusive partner by neglecting your appearance, duties, and responsibilities. This could also be thought of as a type of freezing or fleeing.

It's possible you started yelling at others as a child, because you were screamed at, and responding with a similar energy helped you survive. You became verbally abusive. Now you "get in the face" of anyone who challenges you (or your family). This is a fight response.

Our limbic brain is great at handling acute, immediate stress. If a bear jumps out at you right now (I sure hope this doesn't happen, but if it does, please stop reading, and if it's black, fight back, brown, lie down, and white, well…good night), your limbic brain will kick into action without any logical thought. You'll either punch it, freeze, or start running very quickly.

When I describe a situation as "traumatic," this is what I'm thinking of. It is something that in some way threatened your safety to such an extent that it led to a "trauma response," a fight, flight, or freeze reaction.

Our brains learn very quickly, especially our limbic brains, when it comes to safety and motivation. As I mentioned earlier, if a child touches a hot stove burner, the odds are pretty good they won't touch it again.

The healthy response, of course, is to pay attention to whether the burner is on, and use the stove for cooking, but avoid touching the stove.

However, our limbic responses aren't logical and can overreact to keep us safe. It's possible the child who touched the stove will refuse to go near a stove, or even be afraid of anything related to cooking.

This shows the power of a trauma response to "stay with us." If a dog bit you as a child, you may only vaguely remember the incident, but be afraid of all dogs to this day.

The limbic brain doesn't always distinguish between "this one dog" and "all dogs," and protects us by erring on the side of just avoiding all dogs.

So, now every time you see a dog, your heart races. You freeze. Your face turns red. And you start to panic. You may have no idea why this is happening because it is largely unconscious.

If you have been traumatized in this way, then you may be in a low-key trauma response all the time. Our brains err on the side of overprotection rather than under-protection, so our trauma responses often persist chronically long after the trauma has passed.

Let me explain why. Other animals will experience a form of acute trauma (like getting attacked). And, if they survive, they will soon go back into a more homeostatic state, called the "rest and digest" state. An animal will learn from the event in a very basic way (called "associative learning").

If someone kicks a dog, the dog will likely avoid that person in the future. This is associative learning. However, dogs aren't sitting around ruminating on the experience, the person, or worrying that others may exist like that person.

The human brain can ruminate (cycle through the past) and speculate into the future, meaning that we can worsen the trauma response by triggering ourselves repeatedly when there is no direct danger.

Imagine a wolf was attacked by a bear, and it went home and complained all night about it to its wolf spouse. Then it got on social media and shared photos of how injured it was. Then, the wolf was viewing content on social media all day related to bear attacks throughout the world. And before bed, it was ruminating on the event, and worrying that the streets were filled with bears, and that the wolf government was "going easy" on bears because some wolf politicians were using that as a scary talking point.

The wolf would never get to the "rest and digest" phase because its awareness would be entirely on what was triggering it. The wolf would physiologically be in a low-key fight, flight, or freeze response all day, and experiencing the stress of this.

It would be experiencing constant stomach aches, unexplained pain and illnesses, and much more, as its limbic system is constantly worked up in a stress response.

This is what is happening in our modern world with a lot of situations, but particularly people traumatized by their relationships. This is why you feel chronically stressed, and your physical health is impacted.

My experience on the "toxic relationship" side of TikTok is that many people who have been traumatized in toxic relationships tend to maintain the trauma on a regular basis, despite claiming to not want to.

For example, they will vent about their toxic partner whenever they can. They make angry videos about them. They watch content all day from other people who have been similarly mistreated. They comment on those videos and get into comment debates.

The phrase "my narcissist" gets thrown around a lot, as if it's a badge of honor to outdo other people as to which ex was the most toxic.

While this seems like a way to "heal," if you understand what a trauma response is, this is simply reliving the trauma and making sure the trauma response brain wiring stays persistent.

So, why would someone who doesn't want to feel this way, and who wants to get rid of feelings for their partner or ex, continue to place this person at the center of their mental universe and even pay attention to things that get them emotionally worked up?

I have already discussed how the brain wires and how you can get addicted through the brain's reward system. But there may be something else at play.

Believe it or not, at some level, being in the trauma response seems to relieve the pain of the trauma, so reliving the trauma can feel good. I know this sounds strange, but doesn't it seem like some people feel *more alive* when they are re-telling their traumatic story, or involved in drama related to their toxic partner who has hurt them?

In the seminal book on trauma, The Body Keeps The Score, author Dr. Bessel van der Kolk makes this point. In many of his group therapy sessions working with veterans, he found that the only time they truly lit up and were "alive" is when they were telling their traumatic war stories.

He also mentions a study that found that when traumatized people were re-experiencing their trauma (in this case veterans watching a violent war movie), their body was releasing the equivalent of 8 mg of injected morphine (see page 33)!

In other words, reliving their trauma was making them feel very good at an unconscious level.

I have my ideas about why this is the case, and I'll share it here, and this forms the basis of what I do as a hypnotist to help others.

When you are presented with a stressor of some kind, your

brain and central nervous system want that stress to be relieved. When it happens, your dopamine levels drop, meaning your brain is now motivated to seek the reward of ending the stress.

So, when stress comes, you have two ways to feel this relief. The first is to solve the problem in some way. And, if you can, you do that. You take those steps, and the problem is solved! And, your brain learns that it feels great to take action and solve the problem.

However, if you *don't* know how to solve the problem, or *can't* (for example, your toxic partner is physically restraining you, or you fear they will "punish" you in some way), then the stress doesn't go away. But, you still want to feel the relief of not having the problem anymore.

So, let's say you don't really know how to leave your partner because you share a place together and you don't have a job. This is a real problem that you don't know how to solve. Your dopamine levels are low, and since you haven't removed the problem, your brain goes into a stress response, to motivate you to act. It does this by generating emotions of discomfort, like anger, sadness, etc.

These emotions don't go away simply because you want them to. So, you lash out, yell, scream, or just cry. Because you have done *something* to express these emotions of discomfort, your brain releases some dopamine and endorphins (which bind to the brain's opioid receptors), and you feel better. This is why when you're angry, yelling and screaming feels "good" at some level even though you're angry.

So, your brain is learning that "relief from the problem = entering a stress response" rather than learning that "relief from the problem = doing something about it."

So, you have trained your brain to (as weird as it sounds) feel "good" when responding with a trauma response, because your brain is associating this with some type of relief.

And, this is why we often naturally gravitate toward our trauma response, rather than toward healing or taking meaningful action.

This is also why trauma seems to keep us "stuck," at least in terms of our reptilian and limbic brains. These areas of our brain don't really have a sense of time. Our neocortices understand there is a past and a future. Our limbic and reptilian brains understand the present.

So, if you have been traumatized, and if your limbic brain could speak (it can't very well by the way…maybe in grunts and chirps), it would say "in 2003 what I did worked to protect you from your abusive partner, so it must work today, so let's keep making you feel this way."

So, perhaps you were rejected harshly by your crush at 13. You learned to avoid asking anyone out ever again, a freeze or flight response. Thus, when it comes to rejection, your limbic brain is still stuck as that 13-year-old version of you.

Maybe when it comes to interpersonal relationships, your limbic brain is still that five-year old you, when to deal with your mom's constant belittling, you learned to cope by being overly complimentary and people-pleasing, a type of flight response (by avoiding necessary direct communication).

At that age, when you tried extra hard to compliment and please your unreasonable mom, that response "worked" and felt "good" at some level, and now you do it as an adult.

The same is true of your toxic relationship. If they message you or reach out, it still brings back the trauma responses that you are used to. I'll write more about this in the next chapter.

Chapter 13

Trauma Bonding Part 3: Survival Mode

In this chapter, I want to focus on the impact of trauma and the trauma bond, in terms of what they do to you, and how they have changed your brain significantly. These changes have happened without you even knowing it, since many of them are unconscious.

Almost every client I work with comes to me believing they have "lost themselves," and this is because they are so focused on just getting by that they have no time, energy, and brain space to devote to anything else. This is what happens when you spend so much time dealing with someone toxic.

In this chapter on survival mode, I'll begin by addressing changes to your brain's threat detection system, which becomes dysfunctional thanks to trauma. Some brain structures involved in this include the amygdala, hippocampus, and hypothalamus.

The amygdala receives sensory information from the thalamus and other parts of the brain, and then it sends signals to other areas of the brain to initiate the fight, flight, or freeze response.

Thus, when the amygdala detects a potential threat, it sends a signal to the hypothalamus, which releases stress hormones such as adrenaline and cortisol.

The hippocampus, involved in the formation and retrieval of memories, plays a role in the stress response since it helps encode and consolidate memories of threatening or stressful events.

When you have gone through trauma, your brain is so used to experiencing stress, and so keenly sensitive to avoid any new threat, that you begin to see threats everywhere, including in places where they don't exist.

This is why if you were in a toxic relationship, you now see the world in a "darker" way. You don't trust people anymore, but you may particularly distrust people of the same gender as the person who hurt you. You believe people are mean, bad, not trustworthy, and just waiting to victimize you. You are so sure that this is the case, you may even think it's absurd that anyone actually believes people are pretty good overall.

If someone says something to you, you interpret it as negatively as possible. You take everything personally, and every little thing now "sets you off."

You may even become scared of going out or doing things that you used to feel safe doing. You advertise all of this to the world, and even criticize people who see the world in a more positive way.

Because of this, trauma keeps you stuck in what is often called "survival mode." Put simply, this means you are in a low key "fight, flight, or freeze" response perpetually, and are focused mainly on "getting by" rather than thriving.

This is why if you have been in a toxic relationship, you've likely lost interest in things that aren't essential to survival. You have given up hobbies, lost friends, and no longer enjoy things that you used to.

It's also why you likely have let your physical and mental health slide because you don't have "time" to do the things that build you up physically and emotionally.

You may even be afraid of the places where you could go to get help, like the gym, or a therapist or doctor's office. If you were scared of certain things prior to your toxic relationship, these fears have likely been amplified.

This is essentially a trick of your brain, because you *do* have time, but your brain is so focused on survival, it doesn't allow you to see that there is time to do other things.

When you're surviving, it means you're not thriving, and

there's a reason for this, which I'll discuss in chapter 15. However, first I want to explain how living in survival mode can change who you are and how you act towards others.

Chapter 14

Trauma Bonding Part 4: Turning Toxic Too

There is a much darker side of "survival mode," which I want to outline in this chapter.

One of my acquaintances was dating a woman who had just gotten out of a toxic relationship a year earlier. He was in love with her and knew that she had been through a lot with her previous partner.

She was legitimately the victim of a controlling and abusive person, who cheated on her frequently. However, whenever he described how she treated *him*, it was obvious to everyone that her actions and behaviors were also incredibly toxic.

She frequently went back to her toxic ex, and even kissed him once while she was committed to my friend. She frequently gave my friend "the silent treatment." He made major life adjustments for her, only for her to barely reciprocate. She nearly always backed out of many things she committed to doing, leaving him with major financial and time burdens.

She was very suspicious of him at times, and didn't allow him to have female friends. She occasionally blasted him for little, insignificant things he did. If he ever suggested, even in a calm and neutral way, that she was behaving badly, she would call him a "narcissist just like my ex" and make him feel guilty for even raising the issue.

My friend was infinitely patient, and always explained that she only did it because of "her abusive ex" and because of other issues from her past.

One sad fact of living in survival mode is that it leads to toxic and self-centered behaviors. When you think about it, to survive in a toxic relationship, you must become relatively self-centered yourself.

If this describes you, you know that to survive you often had to lie to yourself and others. You may have enabled your partner's bad behavior for fear that you might be punished. Maybe you got into fights on their behalf or treated others poorly to remain on your toxic ex's good side.

You became needy, because they rarely gave you positive attention. You became emotionally reactive, and frequently yelled and screamed to fight back against them. Or you shut down and checked out.

You became extremely insecure and thus became very suspicious about every little thing your partner did. To stop them from cheating or doing other things, you may have become controlling, insisting they can't see their friends or do hobbies that put them in temptation's way.

In essence, it's possible that you turned into them, or at least a lighter version of them, without even knowing it. And, because you are a legitimate victim, it's very easy for you to explain away these behaviors, and even justify them, based on your past trauma.

So, you may lash out at your current partner, track their every move, insist on spending every second with them, and try to control them, but in your mind, it's okay because of your troubled past.

But isn't this eerily similar to excuses your toxic partner made to justify their toxic behavior?

In plenty of cases, victims of past toxic partners bring these survival behaviors, sometimes called "baggage," into future relationships. They bring neediness, insecurity, suspicion, emotional reactivity, aggressive communication, passive communication, emotional shutting down, and other dysfunctional "strategies."

The problem with this is obvious. The healthy partner you are seeking is not going to put up with these unhealthy strategies for very long. They will hopefully do their best to support you in your healing journey, but after a while, it will be too much for them to handle.

However, let me ask you this: who *will* put up with you using these strategies? Someone who is unhealthy and uses those strategies themselves.

So, it is very important to understand that you may have come out of your toxic relationship with traits that require healing. You can simultaneously be both a legitimate victim and have emerged from that situation with behaviors that are unhealthy.

In later parts of the book, I'm going to explain honestly taking responsibility for your actions, and one area you may have to do this is to acknowledge that you may have developed many toxic habits yourself, some of which might be harming your current relationship and dating opportunities. You may also be using your past, or your current trauma bond with a toxic ex, as excuses for why you have these toxic traits.

CHAPTER 15

TRAUMA BONDING PART 5: YOUR FAULTY FRONTAL LOBE

One day I was talking to a client, and she really wanted to leave a toxic relationship. However, when it came time to talk about leaving, every thought went back to how bad her relationship was.

I said, "what is something that you want to accomplish in life?" She answered, "that's tough, because my toxic ex always stopped me from accomplishing things!"

I tried to get her back to the topic at hand, which was to imagine a future without him.

"So, can you tell me something you can look forward to in a few years after you have gotten over him?" I asked.

She replied, "I mean, maybe seeing my friends, but I haven't looked forward to anything for years. Let me tell you about the time he stopped me from attending a class in college that derailed my entire degree."

"So," I interrupted gently, "you would take classes if you left him? If so that's great!"

"Oh no, I don't think I could ever do that. I bet I'm too old. That's what happens when someone toxic like him totally kills your dreams!"

It was as if her brain was incapable of even imagining a good life, but was still stuck in the "frame" that her toxic ex had established for her. Whenever I tried to get her to imagine a new and great reality, she always brought it back to her old and limiting reality.

If you understand the brain, this makes total sense. When you're stuck in survival mode, and your brain and body are flooded with stress chemicals, the advanced parts of our brains (the neocortex and frontal lobe) become dysfunctional.

Remember, the frontal lobe is responsible for imagining, seeing a way forward, deliberating, seeing future possibilities, and delaying and regulating emotional responses.

Without a functional frontal lobe, you're at the whims of your emotions, you live in the past, and are stuck in old moments. You're unable to imagine anything new, and your old reality is the only reality you can even see.

My client was experiencing every one of these symptoms, and as such was cognitively unable to even imagine a future, let alone take steps to achieve it.

I was able to imagine a better future for her, but she was unable to. Of course, I used hypnosis and other tools to get her to imagine one, but the initial resistance I experienced is very common.

Let me give you a more extreme example that will help this make more sense. Have you ever been in a threatening situation or extreme panic?

When you are in this mode, you can't solve an algebra equation or think creatively. In many cases, you may not even be able to recall logical facts or speak.

About 20 years ago, some local teens were egging cars in my parents' neighborhood. I was living with them at the time, and they had egged cars for two nights in a row. So, I waited on the porch the third night.

Everyone thought "there is no way they were dumb enough to do it again" but nonetheless I waited, believing people dumb enough to egg cars would definitely be dumb enough to do something three times in a row at the same time.

After a few moments, I heard the "crack, crack, crack" of

multiple eggs hitting cars. I sprang into "fight" mode, and ran inside to get the car keys. Next thing I know, my dad, brother, and I were in a car chase with some local teens, and I was driving.

During the drive, we called the sheriff to let them know we had their license plate. When the sheriff asked for my phone number, I couldn't recall it. I literally forgot my own phone number! My dad, who wasn't driving, and thus was in a calmer state, gave him my number.

I didn't understand why at the time, but my brain was in a "fight" response, and my brain's resources and energy were drained from my neocortex and funneled into my limbic and reptilian systems.

If you've been in a cycle of trauma, this is where your brain is most of the time. I'm going to lay out some of the realities that you may find yourself in. If you are a therapist, coach, family member, or friend, you may notice these changes in the person in your life who is addicted to someone toxic.

For one, you may always bring things back to your toxic relationship or partner. Conversations seem to focus on them. Your social media posts focus on them in some way. What you view on social media may focus on them. You find yourself always going back to them in some way, even if is to vent about them.

Second, you may find yourself being highly emotionally reactive rather than deliberative or logical. In other words, your emotions control you constantly. You get angry easily. You get sad easily. You overreact in ways you regret later, but you keep doing it. You see things in a highly negative and dark way. You tend not to delay gratification because of how you react based on emotions.

Third, you may have trouble communicating, since your neocortex is where language is largely processed. You may feel as if you aren't in touch logically with what you feel emotionally. You may feel as if you can never adequately put words to your internal experiences.

Fourth, you may not be able to imagine something good for you or your future. The minute a friend suggests you're worthy, you may say you're not. The moment it's time to plan for your better future, you tell stories of the past. Whenever someone seems interested in you, you insist there is no way that's possible and you dismiss them. You literally have no idea what a better life would look like for you.

Fifth, you may lack creativity to imagine a new version of you. While you have all kinds of creativity when it comes to spying on your partner or covering up for them, when it comes to getting over them or leaving the relationship, you give up easily and are "all out of ideas."

Finally, you may not even know you are in this state and may come up with reasons to deny why this applies to you. Since the neocortex is responsible for self-reflection and conscious awareness, when you are very entangled in emotions, it can be hard to even be aware that this is the case.

Unfortunately, this can sometimes manifest as a resistance to healing and moving on, which limits your desire and motivation to get help.

If you are a healer, family member, or friend you may even be sick of dealing with someone who is addicted to a toxic person. The toxic situation seems so obvious to you, but your friend or client truly is unable to see how their obsession with their toxic ex (whether strongly loving them or hating them, or both) is unhealthy.

This could be one of the hardest chapters to handle. During my time raising awareness about unhealthy relationships, one of the issues I see the most is people who have physically moved on from toxic relationships, but who have not mentally moved on.

They are still emotionally invested in their toxic ex thanks to the trauma bond. And, as I just mentioned, there can be a strong resistance to healing, and a strong urge to continue filling up their mental space with their ex. But, this is just the addiction and trauma bond living in the past.

Sadly, one side effect of being in survival mode is strong resistance to change, and even being hostile to those trying to help you facilitate change. Just watch the show "Hoarders" if you don't believe me.

In many cases, the hoarders are so unable to leave survival mode that they harass and sabotage the very people who love them and are helping them.

I say this because once you realize that the survival mode state you're in has tricked you into resisting healing, you'll be grateful that someone told you that and urged you to heal and move on. Consider me one of those people urging you to embrace healing!

CHAPTER 16

SO, THAT'S A LOT OF BAD NEWS!

Whew, that's a lot of bad news, right? Your brain has changed significantly. Hopefully, what I have written can help you understand how much you have changed. If you are reading this book on behalf of a loved one or client, you now have a sense of how different the person you're trying to help is compared to before their toxic relationship.

I'm not bringing all of this up to be negative. Not in the least. We are done with the bad news. I shared what has happened simply to state where you have found yourself.

But, we aren't going to dwell on it after this, because that is what your brain has been doing for months, years, and even decades.

The next chapters are going to go through some solutions to your addiction. I'm going to cover ways to deal with the brain changes I discussed, so you can go from surviving to thriving.

Please note that this book is not meant to replace the aid of a professional. While the methods listed here can and will change your life, many people in toxic relationships have significant underlying mental issues (including undiagnosed ones). It is important to consult a professional, if needed.

Not only have I applied these same solutions myself, but so have many clients of mine.

Things may seem hopeless, but I promise you they are not. The only reason they seem this way is because you are in survival mode. Once I walk you through new ways to believe, feel, and act, you'll start to move on and enjoy the benefits of a life where you can thrive.

So please keep reading. Your brain is likely going to find the stories of people's toxic relationships and the explanation of your condition way more interesting than working the solutions. So once you start reading about solutions, your brain may suddenly start to get "bored."

Why? Because this response is a part of your old reality. The important part is coming up, and that is to create your new reality through the changes you are going to make. So be sure to pay close attention to what follows.

And, *do something*.

I would much rather you apply one principle that follows than read about all of them and do nothing. If you're like me, it's easy to love the science and philosophy behind all of this. But, the important thing is to take action.

If you are a healer or loved one, these interventions can be useful for you to use or share, individually or in the setting of a support group.

So, let's get started with the good stuff!

Chapter 17

Take Responsibility

A friend of mine has pretty much been in toxic relationships her entire life, and she is barely 30. I've known her since she was young, and from her first relationship in junior high, until one that just ended as I'm writing this, she has found herself only in unhealthy relationships.

The same cycle happens each time. She falls very quickly for a guy. She ignores every red flag because she is so in love. After around two to three years, it becomes too much. The relationship ends. Then she posts on social media about how horrible toxic people are, directing these at her exes.

When you talk to her, she never recognizes that she has a role in the process. She explains that narcissists and toxic people are everywhere, and she has had significant "bad luck" to always keep finding them. It has never occurred to her that some people have never fallen for someone toxic, so maybe it isn't about "luck" at all.

I must be careful writing this chapter because I don't want to "victim blame," which is what happens when you blame victims for what happens to them.

This is not about blaming people who have had bad things happen to them. But, the only way to truly stop the menace of toxic people is to give victims the ability to handle them. Toxic people can be very manipulative and convincing, but so are scammers who con people out of money.

Imagine if someone who was fleeced out of thousands of dollars by a "Nigerian prince" scam just said, "these scammers are so slick, there is nothing I can do!" We know that they would be getting scammed repeatedly. This is what ultimately happens when you fail to take responsibility for your role in your relationships: you are doomed to repeat the scenario.

While it may not be your fault that you fell for someone toxic, or how they treated you, and you may indeed be a victim, it is still your responsibility to deal with the situation you are now in because of it.

Why is it important to take responsibility for your role in your situation? Because you can never fully change anyone else's behavior, but you can always change what you do.

When I was a teacher at a small private school, our basketball team always lost. I felt bad for them, but after each game, the players would always assign blame for why they lost: bad officiating, the crowd was too loud, the crowd was too quiet, the coach made bad calls, and virtually every possible reason except that they didn't play well.

Even if all those things were true in some capacity, the only thing within their control was their own performance. And, this is true of your addiction to your toxic ex. They may indeed be manipulative, good with words, deceptive, clever, and doing things to make your life miserable, like using the legal system against you. They may constantly try to sneakily draw you back into their life. They may have hurt you and know exactly what to say to get you to react.

Sadly, they aren't going to change. If they were going to change…guess what? They would have by now, and you wouldn't be where you are.

They are going to message you at midnight on Saturday while drunk, because that is who they are. They are going to alternate that with being rude and mean, because again, that is who they are. They are going to do things to work you up, because that is what they have done hundreds of times. How *you* handle every difficult situation is up to *you*.

This chapter may be challenging because it requires you to

accept that you have a role in your dating and relationship history and choices. It is challenging because it can bruise your ego to admit this.

But, it is liberating because once you admit this, the locus of control has moved from them to you, and you will no longer be a victim of their whims or your addictive cravings. You will finally be free.

You may be afraid that you'll feel a lot of shame if you admit the truth, but taking responsibility doesn't mean you need to shame yourself or beat yourself up. Please read the next chapter if you are feeling a lot of shame about your past decisions, especially after completing the exercise at the end of this chapter.

So right now, just take some time to commit to taking responsibility. You are no longer a victim, and no longer subject to the manipulations of toxic people. You're in charge…not them.

It is important to make sure to take responsibility in three important areas.

The first is to take responsibility for the things that led you into relationships with toxic people. These may include things like ignoring obvious red flags, prioritizing passion over your morals and values, hanging around with crowds that you know aren't good for you, rejecting people who are nice because you think they are "boring," or other behaviors and attitudes that lead you into the arms of unhealthy people.

The second is to take responsibility for the behaviors you tolerated, enabled, or did that were unhealthy or immoral within your toxic relationship. These may include lying to others, covering up for your partner, taking their side when they were clearly wrong, destroying relationships with friends and family, squandering your own money or that of others, using substances, procuring substances for them, committing criminal acts, etc.

Third, take responsibility for your own toxic behaviors and attitudes, some of which developed from having to survive in your toxic relationship. These may include neediness, insecurity, being controlling, chronic suspiciousness, emotional reactivity, aggressive communication, passive communication, emotional shutting down, lying, etc.

Right now, create spots on paper (or electronically) for each of the three areas I listed above. Beneath each, honestly list the things that you regret that you now take responsibility for. While there is no need to exaggerate, be honest.

Only list actual factual examples, rather than judging yourself. Avoid using a form of the verb "to be," because this is labeling yourself, not listing unhealthy actions. This activity isn't meant to add to your shame, but to acknowledge the truth.

So, write "I tend to fall for 'bad boys' and find nice guys boring" rather than "I'm an idiot when choosing guys."

Keep it factual. Use the phrase "I looked the other way when my girlfriend stole money from my parents," rather than "I'm a pathetic son."

Write "I use the silent treatment a lot with my girlfriend" instead of "I'm a horrible boyfriend."

Hopefully you get the picture.

After writing them down, you may read them aloud and add "I take responsibility for…" before each one.

It could look something like this: "I take responsibility for my insecurity in my current relationship where I constantly check up on my partner to see where they are."

Or you may say "I take responsibility for bringing my children to live in my ex's unsafe home, when I knew going in that they had a prior history of verbally and physically abusing their own children."

Chapter 18

Now Forgive Yourself

Here is an analogy I often use on social media, especially during my live events on TikTok.

Imagine a boxer in the middle of a fight swings at his opponent and misses. And, because he is so ashamed that he missed, he punches himself in the face as hard as he can. And, he continues this practice throughout the match, until, of course, he loses.

If he did this, we'd think that was absurd, but this is how we often respond to ourselves when we think of our past mistakes.

Acknowledging our mistakes and taking responsibility for them is healthy and allows these mistakes to be processed consciously and healthily.

However, shame is taking a mistake that we made, dwelling on it, and then identifying with it as if it is a core part of who we are.

It is healthy to admit making mistakes and lacking clear judgment. Believing you *are* a mistake and that you *are* stupid is not a healthy response.

Many people who have been in toxic relationships alternate between denial of their responsibility within the relationship, and shaming themselves. Both extremes are unhealthy and likely to slow down the healing process and can even promote your addiction.

This is why this chapter is about forgiving yourself. Continually beating yourself up for the past is just going to make it harder to move on and take charge of your life.

Shaming yourself will also lead you to seek emotional relief from your shame, and this often leads you back to addictive behaviors since in your desire to "feel good" you will seek familiar things.

A lot of us are afraid of forgiving ourselves because we fear that if we do, we'll be tempted to go back to the old behaviors we want to avoid.

But, it doesn't work this way. Forgiving yourself frees you from the chains of the past so you can make new choices.

For this chapter, I want you to verbalize that you forgive

yourself. This may seem silly, but go with it. This is one way to cultivate self-forgiveness and compassion. Just imagine in this exercise that the "present you" is addressing the "past you," and offering forgiveness.

For this first exercise, take out the list you made in the previous chapter. Look in the mirror, imagine you are speaking to the past version of you, and say "I forgive you for _____. You did the best you could with the knowledge you had." Fill in the blank with an item you listed previously that you took responsibility for.

Just address all your past regrets and current toxic behaviors one-by-one, until you have worked through all of them.

Another way to both take responsibility and forgive yourself is to make amends for your mistakes. This may include apologizing to family members, friends, co-workers, or whomever was impacted by your decisions.

When you are addicted to someone toxic, it is very easy to neglect a lot of people in your pursuit of that person, which results in ruined relationships.

Making amends, even if it is through communicating your regret and mistakes, can hasten the feeling of self-forgiveness.

A final tool that can help you with self-forgiveness is called "there is no failure, only feedback."

This is a "presupposition" of neurolinguistic programming,

which is a set of strategies to change your mindset.

Basically, this is a way of viewing your past setbacks with a different, more helpful perspective.

It just means that you can view setbacks and mistakes one of two ways. You can view them as "failures" or as valuable feedback for future behavior.

When you view your mistakes as "failures" this creates a shame-based "frame" around them. When you view them as "feedback" you see them as valuable lessons to gain insight about how to take action more effectively in the future.

This may seem like just a minor change, to look at your past in a different way, but it is very powerful. If you learn from the past, and make changes in the present for the future, you never truly "fail."

As we move on, I suggest continuing to both take responsibility for your actions and forgive yourself for them. This is the path of healing and empowerment.

You'll find that as you use these two strategies, you will not only get over the toxic person you're addicted to, but you'll become a much more empowered and happier person.

You'll also begin to take responsibility in other areas of your life, and begin to understand how empowering it is to accept responsibility.

Additionally, the forgiveness you give yourself will spread to forgiving others, which will also help you heal.

Forgiveness is a powerful tool that I will explore in some more detail in chapter 32.

Chapter 19

Correcting Cranial Chemistry

I was initially going to leave out this chapter and the next, for two reasons. For one, the research on brain chemistry is still young, and I don't want to give an inaccurate impression of this reality. And second, brain chemistry is complex, and many of the chemicals work together in ways that are intertwined, so it is difficult to specifically focus on modulating individual chemicals. So, just be aware of all of this when reading these next two chapters.

In chapter nine I mentioned that when you're in love, your brain's rewards systems become messed up. This involves significant changes in dopamine, norepinephrine, and serotonin levels. These changes lead to infatuation, obsession, ignoring red flags, and addiction.

In this chapter, I'm going to explain ways to help you correct this dysfunction, and get your dopamine and serotonin systems back on track.

While I'm going to specifically address dopamine and serotonin, be aware that norepinephrine levels seem to be tied to these other chemicals, and modulating those will provide healthier levels of norepinephrine.

Keep in mind that the interventions that follow are all behavioral and are not going to lead to instant results.

Some pharmaceuticals and supplements may help modulate these chemicals as well. While I believe in the efficacy of both, I'm not going to mention any of them in this book. You can consult your doctor or do your own research if you feel like you need a boost that may be greater than what I am providing here.

Let's start with dopamine. Getting your brain's dopamine system back in order can be a challenge, but many things can help you modulate dopamine.

I want to share the three techniques that psychiatrist Dr. Anna Lembke recommends that can help you reset your dopamine system. She is the author of the book <u>Dopamine Nation</u>.

The first is to give up, or "fast" from what is causing your dopamine issue. This is going to be the hard part. This is going to mean fasting from the things you do to retain access to your ex or partner. See chapter 25 for more details about this.

You may think that checking their social media, texting them occasionally, or venting about them constantly aren't big things, but they are keeping your dopamine system dysfunctional and tied to them.

Every time you check up on them or message them, your dopamine levels are going back up, giving you that "relief" feeling. Remember, this keeps your dopamine receptors downregulated, meaning they will remain in need of more and more dopamine to feel anything.

The more you completely fast from your addiction to this person, the more your dopamine system will reset, and the fewer cravings you will have for them.

As you do this, your receptors will become more sensitive, and other activities (and people) will feel more pleasurable and satisfying. Dr. Lembke recommends 30 days of fasting.

If you can't completely fast from contact with your ex (for example, because you must deal with shared custody of kids), do your best to make the communication "just business." In other words, only focus on the details that need discussed, and avoid any other conversation.

The next intervention she recommends is to invite something difficult or painful into your life (that is also healthy). Focusing on tasks that are difficult or slightly painful can help reset a dysfunctional dopamine system. This is because the balance of dopamine depends on pain and difficulty just as much as it does on feeling good.

What is "painful" but also "healthy?" One way to define these activities is "meaningful effort." Find things to do that are meaningful to you, but that require some effort and discomfort.

This includes activities like intense exercise, cold showers, taking on meaningful, but challenging projects (like repairing something complicated or building something), obstacle course races (like the "Tough Mudder"), and other things that are good for you, but require some effort to get through.

When I ran the Columbus, Ohio half-marathon with my brother last year, we commented on how excited, happy, and focused everyone was. It seemed remarkable that people literally running miles upon miles could be *happy* doing it.

Our dopamine reward system requires effort and difficulty to be regulated properly. Many people who have been addicted to toxic people have given up doing things that require meaningful effort.

Finally, she recommends radical honesty, with yourself and others. Telling the truth stimulates the frontal lobe and connects the advanced parts of your brain to the pleasure and pain dopamine pathways. This is one effective way to get more conscious control of the dopamine system rather than being controlled by it. This aligns with what I mentioned earlier about "taking responsibility."

Another way to fix your brain's broken dopamine system is to start to fill your life with things that make you feel rewarded and motivated that *aren't* your toxic partner or ex.

One thing that can help you is embracing novelty, meaning that you do and try new things (if they require meaningful effort, even better!).

This facilitates the release of dopamine. Have you ever gotten a new opportunity or had something to look forward to, like a concert? On those days, you just easily wake up, get out of bed, and are highly motivated to get through the day. This is a great example of what I'm outlining.

If you have been in a toxic relationship for a long time, you probably have fewer and fewer things like this to look forward to. In fact, you likely haven't done anything significantly new in months or years.

One trauma response you can develop from being with someone toxic is to rigidly stick to routines. You may even be averse to doing new things and taking risks, making embracing new things in your life difficult.

When I first got out of an addictive romantic situation, one very important step I took was to simply let myself do new things. I drove to new places, went to new restaurants, and took new routes when driving. I allowed myself to explore new clothing styles and activities.

I did this to "find myself" in a way, and put myself out there a little more, but looking back it was a great way to reset my dopamine system. My brain's reward system was tied to my ex, and by doing a bunch of new things, my brain was rewarded by these new activities rather than her.

And it worked very well. I know you may be thinking that doing new things is "pointless" and "too easy" to be an actual solution, but that is just the trauma response telling you this.

Also, exercise has been shown to help raise dopamine levels, whether through the "meaningful effort" mechanism I mentioned above, or maybe through different mechanisms. So, if you don't exercise regularly already, this could be a good option. Some research suggests that exercising outside provides even more of a mental boost.

There are ways to potentially modulate your serotonin system, as well. As I mentioned earlier, some research has shown that serotonin levels go down when you're "in love." Also, the stress and abusive nature of toxic relationships can cause serotonin levels to become unbalanced.

Research in other primates and animals suggests that serotonin levels may rise with accomplishment and status, and diminish with setbacks or loss of status (13). Not only that, but if researchers artificially raise serotonin levels in primates, they begin to behave in ways that increase their status.

While it isn't fully proven, it is possible that accomplishing something and experiencing a rise in status can help raise your serotonin levels (likely dopamine as well).

This is why it is important to get some "wins" if you are stuck on a toxic ex or partner. After I got out of an addictive romantic relationship, my friends were great in that they helped me get some of these "wins."

We went out and they helped me socialize, meet new people, and encouraged me to increase my business activity. It felt great to feel accomplished. It is easy after you have felt a lot of defeat to start to believe you aren't capable of winning. To get some "wins," just focus on small things that you can accomplish.

Take a class, get a project going, or have a friend help you set up a profile on a dating app (if you are ready for this in the healing process). Any "wins" you get that aren't associated with the person you're addicted to can help. See chapter 23 for more information on this.

In this chapter, I focused on modulating some of the "in love" chemicals. Now, I want to move on and explain how to work with some of the long-term bonding chemicals.

Chapter 20

Breaking The Bonds

I mentioned in chapter 10 that we long-term bond through two chemicals primarily, oxytocin and vasopressin. Women seem to typically bond through oxytocin and men more through vasopressin.

In this chapter, I'm going to explain some potential ways to hack your brain to break the long-term bonding you have with someone toxic. I want to mention that what I'm going to explain is speculative, which is to say, not proven. Nothing in this chapter is harmful, so it is worth a try even if it isn't fully proven.

I'm going to start by focusing on vasopressin. High vasopressin levels in the brain are associated with territorial and aggression in animals, and may lead to similar behavior in humans, as I mentioned earlier in the book.

In animals, social support and environmental enrichment may help reduce aggressive behavior due to high vasopressin and the same may be true in humans.

If you are very territorial with someone toxic, interventions such as therapy, coaching, and support groups can help. The support of friends can help, as can making environmental changes (such as being around people who are nurturing). The changes discussed later in this book can help you cool your territorial emotions and automatic responses.

There is quite a bit more research on oxytocin and its role in the brain. So, I'll spend a little more time on this.

Oxytocin gets released under various circumstances, and not all of them are related to romance. However, some are, like cuddling, touching, and kissing.

To facilitate the release of oxytocin in ways that aren't related to your toxic partner or ex, there are things you can do.

One thing you can obviously do is start to put yourself out there romantically, to meet someone who isn't your ex. This is up to you and depends on where you are in the healing process.

If you have a history of dating toxic people or making poor dating decisions, then I suggest you tread carefully if you are looking for someone new to date or make a connection with. You could very easily trade a bond with one toxic person for another.

However, if you believe you are ready, then meeting someone new that you really like is a great way to remove bonding feelings with an ex. However, this brings with it a lot of issues, including that if you are already chemically bonded to your ex or current partner, your brain is likely going to resist finding anyone else attractive or worthy of your time.

Another way to release oxytocin is to form social bonds with others. Oxytocin is released whenever you establish relationships that involve trust and vulnerability. Most people I know who are stuck on someone toxic have "nuked" their social relationships over the years and have nobody close to them, except their toxic partner or ex.

Reach out to friends, family, and people you have neglected socially and start to cultivate those relationships. Take an open attitude towards meeting new people. One tragedy of being with someone toxic is that it makes you lack trust and become skeptical of *all* social opportunities, which ironically just keeps your brain stuck on the toxic person.

Finally, testosterone seems to block oxytocin release in the brain. This may be why men (and likely women as well) with higher testosterone levels are more likely to cheat (14).

So, one way to potentially break the bond with your partner is to increase testosterone levels. Various factors lead to increased testosterone. There are drugs and supplements that may increase levels, but I am not recommending them here, and I'm not sure if any doctor would dare give you testosterone to move past social bonding.

Things that seem to naturally increase testosterone levels include losing weight if you're overweight or obese, sprinting, chopping wood, and weightlifting.

As you can see from this chapter, there aren't necessarily a lot of things you can directly do to attack that long-term bond. The good news is that many of the other things I'm going to explain can help you indirectly address the bonding that has happened. So, let's move on!

Chapter 21

Re-Wiring Your Brain

In 2010, I started making many changes in my life that I now just take for granted. Many of the tools I use with clients, including hypnosis, I put into practice myself. I changed so significantly that I barely remember the way I used to think, feel, and act.

This happened because I literally rewired my brain. I made new neural connections, extinguished old ones, and I became a very different person. I view it almost like a software upgrade, and it was a major one.

If you want to break free from your addiction to a toxic ex or partner, you are going to have to rewire your brain. Like I mentioned previously, our brains are *neuroplastic*, which means we can rewire them. The good news is that it is very possible. The bad news is that it was much easier for you to do this when you were a child, when your brain was naturally extremely plastic. Rewiring your brain as an adult is possible but will be met with more resistance.

The first step to rewiring your brain is to recognize that most of the sensations and thoughts that you have are a result of your old wiring. They aren't "real." They are just a result of what you have done and experienced before.

When you wake up in the morning and feel a strong desire to stalk your ex on social media, that is your old wiring at work. When you find yourself seeing something on their account that makes you upset, that is your wiring at work.

Other people scroll by and see what your ex is posting, but they don't even notice or care, right? The reason you care so deeply is because your brain is wired to do this, thanks to so much previous emotion and repetition, as I mentioned in chapter seven.

When they post something that you assume is about you, and you get angry and feel the strong desire to immediately text them something to defend yourself, that is your old wiring.

This may blow your mind. You may say, "but I *have* to get mad when I see something my ex posts!" or "I *have no choice* but to yell and scream at my ex when he calls because he disrespects me!"

You only believe these things because you have "memorized"

these behaviors for so long that they are firmly wired into your brain. In the same way riding a bike is now easy and automatic for you if you learned as a child, overreacting to this person is now easy and automatic. Those automatic sensations of anger, jealousy, resentment, or even approval-seeking are wired into your brain based on your past.

If you begin to take a new course of action towards your ex for long enough, this new path will eventually become just as automatic as your current path has become.

For this chapter, I just want you to become aware of how your brain is working this way. To do it, you can simply observe all the automatic sensations that come your way. You'll find that most of what you think, feel, and do aren't consciously chosen, but just come to you automatically.

Right now, I want you to think of the person you're addicted to, and just take a few moments to observe all the sensations that come your way. Just observe them as if you are an outsider. This ability is a human mental superpower, by the way.

Even though you consciously want to be done with them, you may have gotten a sensation of sadness, anger, or rage. You may have felt it in your body somewhere, particularly your heart or gut.

Maybe you got a sensation that you miss them. Maybe you now want to check up on their social media. Who put those sensations in there? Your old brain wiring did it!

In the next chapter, I'm going to give you a powerful protocol that can help you rewire your brain to a new reality where you aren't addicted to this toxic person, so you can create new brain wiring that will turn your toxic ex into someone you view neutrally.

For now, just practice getting in touch with the sensations that come to you. As they come, observe them, and recognize they are products of your past.

Chapter 22

The 7-Step Creation Protocol

If you are addicted to a toxic person, you are more than likely in survival mode, as I mentioned in chapter 13. You're emotionally reactive and stuck inside your trauma bond.

The opposite of survival mode is what I (and others) call "creation mode," which is when you are no longer preoccupied with getting by, and are now able to focus on creating the reality that want.

As an analogy, imagine someone running from a tiger, scared for their life, or someone freezing so as not to be seen by an intruder trying to harm them. As I mentioned earlier, could either of these two people paint a masterpiece or develop a new mathematical formula under these circumstances? Absolutely not.

And, when you persist in your survival brain wiring, the same is true of your life. You will never create the life you want if the thoughts and feelings that you consistently entertain keep you stuck in survival responses.

I developed a process called "The 7-Step Creation Protocol." This is a process that will help you re-wire your brain by "waking up" to your automatic thoughts and reactions, and replacing them with a new path that will create new brain wiring.

I have broken this down by steps, and will provide some clear examples of how to do this.

Step 1: Identify your triggers

We default to automatic thoughts, feelings, and actions based on external stimuli, i.e. triggers. We laugh at a pet who hears a can opener and then gets excited as if they are being fed, but we do the exact same thing with associations in our environment.

Unfortunately, toxic people in our lives trigger us to think, feel, and do things that aren't helpful and that keep us stuck in the problem.

This step is simply about recognizing when an external stimulus may send you down a path you don't want to go down. If you can understand what triggers you, then this entire process will be much easier than if you are unaware of your triggers.

For example, a trigger may be that your toxic ex messages you, or that you are sitting around the house bored with nothing to do.

The trigger is what starts you down the path toward repeating the patterns that keep you stuck. So, the trigger of your ex messaging you may send you down the following path based on previous brain wiring: to drop what you're doing and become angry. You may then immediately take it out on your kids or send your ex paragraphs of angry texts.

Or maybe the trigger is that when you're bored at 11:00 PM on weekends, you always message your toxic ex for their attention. This often leads to you low-key falling for them again, or spiraling into sadness, which lasts into the next week.

Step one is about becoming aware of the people and events that are likely to put you in a triggered state, so you can approach these situations proactively. Now that you are aware of potential triggers, move to step two.

Step 2: Pause

Pausing is the most important step of this protocol, even though it is the simplest step. Pausing allows the unconscious path you're taking on autopilot to become conscious. It allows you to activate your frontal lobe.

If you don't pause, you'll continue down the path you have

always taken. The trigger will cause your usual dysfunctional and reactive path through time to happen.

So, if you feel yourself going down the familiar, but disempowering, path based on a trigger, pause for a moment.

Have you ever been driving a route you're familiar with? You are kind of "zoned out" on autopilot, but then something jumps out in front of you and suddenly you become conscious and alert? Similarly, this "pause" step causes you to awake from your autopilot mental slumber.

Step 3: Observe your thoughts, feelings, and sensations

After the trigger, your brain is going to flood you with sensations, feelings, and thoughts based on whatever you have sensed, felt, and thought before.

After you have paused, now you are consciously aware and "awake." You now can observe the sensations arising in you, and determine whether these sensations are in alignment with the best version of yourself, or whether they aren't.

Be sure to observe sensations throughout the body as well as the mind. You may, for example, feel sensations in your heart, gut, or other areas.

You are now poised to become the creator of your own destiny. Keep in mind as you do this, especially initially, the "pull" to just go ahead and repeat old patterns will be strong.

However, the more you practice this, the more you'll be able to separate your automatic sensations from "you." This step is intentionally activating your brain's frontal lobe, and will strengthen your brain's executive function so you are not controlled by your addictive cravings.

So, let's go back to our examples. After your ex texted you, you start to feel that flood of anger and resentment. Your stomach gets tense as well. However, instead of immediately going down the path of automatic behavior, you pause, and observe that you are feeling anger and your thoughts are moving you to take it out on your kids and text your ex back.

Or, it's 11:00 PM on a Saturday, and you have nothing to do. You pause and consciously observe that you are feeling lonely and bored, and your automatic thought is that you should really message your ex to relieve your boredom.

Step 4: Acknowledge and accept the sensations, thoughts, and feelings

This step is to just accept that you really do feel or think this way. This may seem like a minor point, but resisting an uncomfortable thought or feeling just causes it to persistently return, whereas accepting these allows them to pass.

One study found that the only way to get rid of uncomfortable sensations or thoughts was to accept them, rather than fight them. In that study, fighting the sensations just caused them to return over-and-over again (15).

In this step, you are just honestly acknowledging what's going on inside you, accepting that it's happening, and being content with this.

Note that accepting that you're thinking and feeling a certain way doesn't mean you're agreeing it's good, moral, or what you wish you thought and felt. As you'll see, this process doesn't keep you stuck in these thoughts, feelings, and sensations, but rather allows you to move beyond them.

When I use this with clients, I often have them simply say "this is _____, and I accept that I am having this sensation" and fill in the blank with what they are sensing.

In my first example, you may verbalize "this is anger and resentment and I accept that I am having these feelings" or "this is an urge to text-fight with my ex and I accept that I am having this thought."

In my second example, you may verbalize "this is boredom and a craving to reach out to my ex, and I accept these sensations."

Step 5: Label the sensation or thought as unhelpful and a product of your past

This step further allows you to separate the automatic sensations coming your way from "you." In this step, you are taking a moment to label the sensation as unhelpful to you, and you can attribute it to past brain wiring being sent to you automatically.

This step contains elements of Cognitive-Behavioral Therapy and is similar to one step in Dr. Jeffrey Schwartz's Four-Step intervention for OCD, which has a re-labeling component.

Using the first texting example above, you can now label your strong desire to yell at your kids and text-fight with your ex as unhelpful, and just a product of your past because you have done it so many times.

The same is true of the second example. You can acknowledge that your desire to interact with your ex to relieve your loneliness is unhelpful and a result of the fact you have done it that way many times before.

Step 6: Relax using a "physiological sigh" (or other breathing)

When you are in survival mode, remember that your emotional brain is focused on survival. This deactivates your frontal lobe and causes you to be singularly focused on surviving and blinded by emotion.

Thus, you will be very reactive and stuck in the past. The good news is that every step so far has had the effect of allowing your reactive state to cool down and pass, but this step will speed that up.

To move beyond this state, it is important to tell your brain and body that everything is "okay," so your reptilian and limbic brains can chill out. Once they calm down, resources in your brain can be directed away from surviving and towards more creative endeavors.

Dr. Andrew Huberman, whom I mentioned earlier, recommends using what is called the "physiological sigh" to relax. The reason it is so effective is that this is the process the body intuitively does *after* going through something stressful or frightening.

By doing it, you are signaling to your unconscious mind that the stress has ended, and it will reduce its physiological stress response accordingly to reflect this, even if the stress actually hasn't passed.

Here is how to do it. Take two deep inhales through the nose (with no exhale in between) and then do a full exhale out of your mouth until your lungs are empty.

Do two of these or as many as is needed. This is telling your brain and central nervous system that it is okay to relax. This step will further help you exit a state of stress and ready your brain for the next step.

If you have other breathwork you prefer, please feel free to use that here instead.

Step 7: Direct your attention to doing something that is more empowering

The final step is to pay attention differently, in a way that will lead you to a new reality that is better aligned with what you want from your life.

So far, "The 7-Step Creation Protocol" has allowed you to: recognize potential triggers, pause so you can become consciously "awake," observe your sensations, accept them so they do not persist, label them as an unhelpful product of your past, and modulate your central nervous system to relax.

Now comes the fun part…creating a new reality (and new brain wiring) so you are no longer stuck in your old habits, and beginning to "practice" new ones so they will become your future automatic sensations. This could include leaving behind potentially unhealthy survival behaviors you developed that turn off healthy partners, which I mentioned previously.

At this point in the protocol, ask yourself, "what is a more empowering and helpful path I can take?"

The sky is the limit, especially if your frontal lobe is becoming healthier! You are no longer stuck in old patterns, but now free to explore all sorts of new, creative, and exciting possibilities, including new ways to feel, think, and act!

Let's say that text message from your ex comes in. You may decide that a better path is to call a friend, have a good laugh at how ridiculous your toxic ex is, and just ignore them.

So, you call your friend, and not only are your kids happy you're not taking it out on them, you also haven't wasted your time text-fighting with your ex. Instead of being worked up for hours afterwards, you feel happy because you had a good laugh.

It's 11:00 AM on a Saturday morning, and you know that at 11:00 PM you'll be bored and triggered to reach out to your toxic ex. So, you decide to proactively look for things to do. You notice there is a "wine and paint" event locally that starts at 9:00 PM and goes until 11:30 PM.

You invite a friend, and she agrees to go with you. You are painting and enjoying yourself until it ends. You had so much fun, you're exhausted. You go home and go straight to bed. You even met some cool new people at the event.

Look at the very different realities you created in the two examples above. You have not only created new realities, but you have begun the process of telling your brain that these new paths are "normal" as you pair them with emotion and hopefully repeat them.

Now, in the future, your brain will entertain different, healthier options as a "new" normal, and eventually you will default to these new, more empowering strategies.

When you are stuck in survival mode, you do the same things repeatedly. But, when you are in creation mode, you have all kinds of amazing options at your disposal.

The more you use this protocol, the more you'll get creative and do things you never expected possible! And the more your life will change!

One thing to keep in mind is that the old brain wiring you have is likely very strong. I mentioned previously that the more often you experience something the more firmly it is wired into your brain.

Establishing new connections requires practice. To create new habits related to a toxic person you're addicted to will require you to "memorize" a new reality in the same way you learned to ride a bicycle. It may be awkward at first. You may need to use tools to make it easier (kind of like training wheels). This book contains plenty of tools you can use, and I'll explain more of them in the next chapters.

And, you may fall off a lot and have to get back on. And you will have to do it again.

During some moments it may feel awkward, but once again,

the feeling of it being "awkward" is just your old wiring coming out.

"The 7-Step Creation Protocol" isn't magic that will always work every single time, especially early on, but it will work when applied regularly. You may also be thinking that this protocol can apply to other areas of your life, including eating better, finding a new job, or other areas of your life where you're stuck.

You are absolutely correct! If you thought this, then congratulations, your frontal lobe is working and already exploring possibilities.

Chapter 23

The Confidence-Accomplishment Spiral

Here is a tool that can help you create new neural connections in your brain and feel better and better about the changes you're making!

When I work with clients, I almost always start small. Most people I work with have had their self-confidence shredded over the years, and at an unconscious level, they truly believe they are incapable of accomplishing much. When you have dealt with toxicity for months and years (and decades), you can feel worthless and incapacitated.

Jonathan and I have a tool that we call the "confidence-accomplishment spiral" which we developed with our friend and colleague Joshua Wagner. The opposite could be thought of as the "insecurity-failure spiral."

Look at it like this. The more you accomplish, the more confident you become. The more confident you become, the more you are motivated to accomplish more things, which then makes you even more confident. And, it just keeps going up from there. This is why already-confident people are so great at accomplishing things.

The opposite is also true, and this may be your reality after your unhealthy relationships. You've been beaten down, belittled, and abused, and this makes you feel horrible about yourself. And because you feel horrible, you're reluctant to act proactively, and you do nothing. Because you're reluctant to do anything, you feel even more horrible.

As I mentioned in the chapter on brain chemistry, when you have been with someone toxic, you haven't had a lot of "wins." Paradoxically, you need wins to have the confidence to get wins.

This is why it is important to start to accomplish something, even if it is small, and then relish those accomplishments a little. This sets the spiral into action, which will build your confidence and allow you to break the cycle of going back to your toxic ex or partner (and feeling defeated in general).

If you are trying to help a friend or client in an addictive situation, you can help them get wins. In fact, they may need your support because they can't even begin to see a way to get out of their negative spiral.

Offer to go out and help them meet some new people. Set up a dating profile for them (if they are ready). Go shopping with them to get some new clothes. Work on a project together. Go to a concert together. Be their workout buddy.

Do *something* to get some wins and accomplishments. Enroll in a 5k a few months out and train for it. Join a local sports league. Look into auditioning for a play with a local civic theater. Take acting or dance lessons.

You can also simply do small tasks that can start to build your confidence, like smiling at strangers or even moving to saying "hi" to them.

Unfortunately, if you have been addicted to someone toxic, your confidence has been sapped, and you likely have accomplished less than you are capable of. Now is the time to reclaim both!

Chapter 24

Restoring Balance

A friend of mine has this habit of disappearing off the face of the earth when he gets a girlfriend. Before he gets into a relationship, he's social, hanging out, doing a lot of cool things, and then once he is partnered up…poof…he's gone.

He gains weight, stops doing things that keep him healthy, and he makes his girlfriend his entire world. Then, when he inevitably gets broken up with (because he turned into someone unattractive), he starts to regain the balance in his life that he lost. Then the cycle just repeats.

Honestly, I'm not even describing just one particular person, but nearly every person I know who has gotten into relationships over the years. Those weren't even toxic relationships per se, so imagine how easy it is to lose balance when you are in a toxic relationship!

This chapter is about restoring the balance that you lost thanks to your addiction to someone toxic. When you're addicted to someone like that, your life changes dramatically. You are so focused on dealing with the chaos that a toxic person brings into your life that everything else goes by the wayside.

When I work with clients, restoring balance is a key part of breaking that addiction.

Almost everyone I know who is addicted to someone toxic is used to that person being their entire world. Whether it's to cover up for them, be obsessed with them, or even vent about them constantly, the toxic person has become the center of their metaphorical universe.

In this section, I'm going to give you ways to restore balance. I know quite a few people who have rarely, if ever, been single since their early teenage years, and many of them have dated toxic people for most of their lives.

One client I worked with is in her thirties and is literally single for the first time since she was 11! If this describes you, then you may not be restoring balance, but finally *developing* some balance that you never had.

Whether you are restoring balance, or finally getting some, this section will benefit you tremendously. If you are reading this book to help a loved one or client, you can encourage them to get some balance and help them out.

Balance can be restored in the following areas: physical health, mental health, social health, spirituality, recreation and hobbies, self-development and education, finances, and civics.

These all overlap in many ways. For example, taking care of your physical health impacts your mental health. So, focus on coming up with some ideas in each category even if it may seem irrelevant to you.

For this chapter, write out ways you can take charge of each of these areas. I'm going to define each briefly and give you some suggestions.

Physical Health

Many of my clients gained a lot of weight while being in a toxic relationship, while others lost too much weight and were dangerously thin. Many gave up exercising and eating right, and instead ate irregularly, snacked a lot, or used things like alcohol and marijuana as coping mechanisms.

Many also failed to maintain regular visits to doctors and dentists, let their gym memberships lapse, or neglected other areas of physical health maintenance.

Restoring the balance of your physical health could look like this: exercising more, getting your diet under control, preparing and cooking healthy meals, or reducing (or eliminating) your use of coping substances.

It may mean getting to the doctor or dentist for conditions or problems you have put off and not addressed. It may mean rejoining the gym, or even finding a way to get health insurance coverage if you have neglected that.

You'll find that getting your physical health back in balance will positively shape other aspects of your life.

Mental Health

When you're with someone toxic, it is obvious your mental health suffers. It is also common to ignore daily routines that keep you mentally healthy, like meditation, taking mental health medications, or meeting with professionals.

Getting your mental health balanced may mean starting a meditation practice, scheduling an appointment with a therapist, doctor, or coach, or addressing addictions that you have left untreated (including by attending AA or NA meetings).

You may need to focus on stress reduction or learning techniques like many of the ones shared in this book. You may also need to develop routines that focus on self-care and self-love.

Social Health

I don't have to explain how easy it is to neglect your social health when you're in a toxic relationship. Close relationships with friends, family, and even having a network of acquaintances are very important for happiness and well-roundedness.

Months and years of isolation that come from being with someone toxic can decimate your social network, and I'm not referring to people on social media. I am talking about real world connections. While I'm not dismissing the value of internet connections, I'm saying it is easier to neglect more significant, real world, relationships while in a toxic relationship.

One major way to get your social health together is reaching out to friends that you have neglected. After I got out of a bad relationship, I reached out to friends I hadn't seen in years. I had to travel a little to see some of them, but they were very glad to meet and catch up. It was extremely helpful in my healing process.

You can also focus on repairing friendships and family relations that may have soured because of your toxic relationship. This is where being honest and upfront can be helpful, by acknowledging the mistakes you made in prioritizing someone toxic over people close to you.

You can also work on getting out more and networking to make new social connections. After my breakup, I went to places to just hang out, like coffee shops, parks, or breweries. I talked to the people near me and got to know them, just to make a connection. They are still my friends and acquaintances to this day.

Spirituality

Most of my clients have neglected their spirituality while in a toxic relationship. Spiritual practices can often take a "back seat" to addictive behaviors and cravings. Also, it's very likely that you compromised many of your values and ethics to be with someone toxic, which further weakened your spiritual life.

Restoring spiritual balance is very important if you are a spiritual or religious person, but can be helpful even if you aren't. Spirituality doesn't have to involve anything supernatural, and can be about connecting to something bigger than yourself, or even finding a grounding in the "everyday."

If you are religious, this can involve getting back to your house of worship more regularly, or resuming your meditation, prayer, or devotional practices.

It could mean attending groups at your house of worship for people struggling with relationship issues. It may involve going through rituals that are helpful for healing, like going to confession if you are Catholic or Orthodox.

If you aren't religious, you can find things to do that provide purpose and meaning. You can even explore religious or spiritual practices that align with your beliefs, or explore secular philosophies that have meaning, like Stoicism or a more secular expression of Buddhism.

Spirituality is very subjective, so it will vary depending on the person, but for this section, focus on adding things to your life that give you purpose and meaning in alignment with your values and religious tradition.

Recreation and Hobbies

When you are with someone toxic, you often give up things that you do for fun. There isn't "time" for a lot of fun when you're surviving or scared all the time.

My clients often say things like, "I *used to* go to concerts all the time," or "*in the past*, I loved to hike" or whatever else used to make them feel alive.

When they're first meeting with me, they no longer have "time" to do the things that enliven them and make life worth living, which is a sad reality of having spent a lot of time with someone toxic and draining.

Americans often think recreation doesn't matter, which is why so many have a poor work-life balance, but it does. Doing things that you enjoy just for fun is very important for your wellbeing.

If you're addicted to a toxic ex or partner, you're used to

getting your happiness from that person, just used to feeling miserable all the time, or both. Recreational activities can help you feel good and enjoy life without this person.

So, here is your chance to prioritize recreational activities. You know all those things that you said *used* to give you pleasure? Those things you have been saying you'll get around to doing? Now is your chance to prioritize them!

Ideas include hiking, golfing, sports leagues, art activities, concerts, festivals, seeing friends, traveling, retreats, playing an instrument, or even a few spontaneous trips to random places.

Maybe you can get back together with the folk band you left when became "too busy" because of your toxic relationship. You can pull out your glove and bat and look for a softball league. Or, you can start painting again.

The sky is the limit! Remember, if you're creating rather than surviving, there are many things that you can do!

One thing to keep in mind is that you can do things by yourself! One limiting attitude many of my clients have when we first meet is that they can't do certain activities alone because it is "weird." This includes fun activities like going to concerts, visiting restaurants or bars, etc. Yes, you can! In fact, doing things you enjoy alone is a great way to heal and grow as a person.

Self-Development and Education

Most people I know who have been with someone toxic have given up self-development and educational opportunities for their toxic partner. They dropped out of college. They changed majors. They took jobs they hated instead of pursuing their dreams. Now is the time to reclaim these!

It is never too late to focus on your development, whether formal (like college) or informal (like taking classes on Udemy or just reading books on positive change).

Many community colleges and career centers have adult education programs that are relatively inexpensive. There are certifications out there on Udemy and Coursera, and a bunch of classes on the Internet.

Even by reading this book, you're focusing on your self-development which is good!

Come up with some educational opportunities that you would like to pursue. Give yourself permission to call your local college or career center and see what options they have. Take a low-cost class to learn a new skill.

Developing yourself, even just a little, can have amazing benefits and give you purpose and fulfillment. This will definitely help you lessen your dependence on the person you're addicted to.

Finances

When you're in a toxic relationship, you often lose financial balance for multiple reasons. For one, many toxic partners are "financial drains," because they often refuse to work, but have expensive habits, addictions, and legal fees.

Also, if you're in a toxic relationship, you often cope by spending money. This includes eating out frequently, using substances, shopping too much, etc.

Plus, when you're in "survival mode," you don't really have the time and focus to learn about money, start a business, or think about investing. You're mainly just worried about paying bills on time and hoping you don't get kicked out of your apartment because your toxic partner did something dumb again.

Getting your finances back in balance is exciting, because when you start seeing money in your account, it feels much better than living paycheck to paycheck! And, this extra money can be used to help you get balance in other areas, such as going back to school, getting needed dental work, or paying for the gym.

Here are a few ways to get your finances together. Start learning about money and investing. Even a few basic articles can help you begin to understand how they work, and the more you know, the more you're in charge of your financial future.

Focus on paying down credit card bills or any bills you're

behind on, where late fees and penalties are adding up. Look into debt consolidation or bankruptcy options if you are in extreme financial distress (but be sure to research these options carefully to avoid scammers).

I highly suggest creating a budget with the input and commitment of anyone in your household. Even if it is basic, it's good to know where your money is going.

Look into making little changes that add up after a while. Adjusting the temperature in your house a few degrees can add up to hundreds of dollars of savings a year, as can buying generic options at the grocery store instead of name brands.

Explore investment and high-interest savings accounts. As of 2023, the Robinhood app makes investing easily accessible, and there are many online savings accounts with competitive rates that have no minimum balance or monthly fees (if none of this makes sense, then read a few articles so it begins to make sense).

Instead of eating out all the time (and even worse, door-dashing), make a trip to the grocery every week with some meal ideas in mind. If you're addicted to something that costs you a lot of money (like substances, video games, or shopping) focus on getting help for those addictions the same way you are getting help for your addiction to someone toxic.

Civics

Finally, let's discuss civics. This is going out into your community and making a difference. Many organizations need volunteers, and this is a great way to feel good, positively impact the world, and even meet great new people.

You can volunteer at animal shelters, places of worship, hospitals, and more. Take the initiative and call around to places (or check out their websites) to see who needs people and what opportunities are available.

You could even volunteer to help support others who have struggled within toxic and abusive relationships.

Hopefully as you do this chapter's activities to restore balance in your life, you are feeling excited. Getting balance in your life is essential to moving on from someone toxic, but also living a full and rich life.

Being someone who lives a rich and full life is highly attractive to other people who are living rich and full lives. So, doing this will make you more attractive to healthy and balanced potential partners.

Chapter 25

Limit Access

When I bring tortilla chips into my house, I know I'll eat a lot of them, and go off my healthy eating plan. I've tried to have them in my house and eat them in moderation, but when that bag is sitting there, it's egging me on to eat every chip inside during one sitting.

If they are in my house, to borrow a Star Trek quote, "resistance is futile." So, I keep them out of my house entirely. If my daughter wants them, I have her keep them in her room, out of sight.

Research shows that when you have easy access to something you're addicted to, you're way more likely to indulge that addiction (16). This is one reason the opioid epidemic exploded in the United States. Doctors were encouraged to widely prescribe opioid painkillers, and gladly did so, getting many people hooked on them.

In most of the recent past, like when I was growing up in the 1980s, it was very difficult to stay connected to a toxic ex. Contacting someone wasn't very convenient. You could have called them on a landline phone, stopped by their house or job, or maybe mailed them a letter.

However, finding the phone number or address of someone you knew in the past could have proven difficult, especially if they got an unlisted number. If you stopped to see them at work enough, it's possible you could have been thrown out and barred from returning.

It was also challenging to keep up with what an ex was up to. Knowing most of the details of their life and relationships would have been nearly impossible.

You wouldn't have been able to see their jealousy-inducing vacation photos, or have access to their passive-aggressive offhand remarks that were clearly about you.

You likely wouldn't even have known whom they were dating, unless you saw them while they were on a dinner date, or heard details through the local gossip grapevine.

For better or worse, unless you were willing to follow an ex like a private detective (or hire one), you had very little access to them or what was happening in their life. Because of this, it was much easier to move on and not continually indulge your addiction.

This limited access in effect created a forced dopamine fast, which would have helped an addicted person's dopamine system normalize, and make moving on easier.

However, since the advent of the internet and social media, if you're addicted to someone toxic, you now have unprecedented access to your "drug of choice." And, they have unprecedented access to you.

You can literally spend your entire day indulging your addiction. This includes activities like stalking your ex's social media to see every detail of their life, or messaging them through text or on social media.

You can also find potentially millions of outlets that allow you to wallow in your addiction and become constantly triggered.

Whereas in the past, it took some effort in terms of time and energy to get in contact with an ex, today, contact is often as simple as sending a five-second text or making a brief comment on a social media status of theirs or one of their friends.

Basically, modern technology enables you to spend most of the day focused on your toxic ex or partner. If you carry your smartphone with you constantly, you can even indulge your addiction while you're supposed to be working, studying, exercising, enjoying your hobbies, or worshiping God.

You're not even safe from this addiction while you sleep! Thanks to the ability to precisely customize smartphone notifications, your phone can even ding and vibrate to awaken you from slumber so you can see what an ex might have recently posted.

So, it is absolutely crucial that you get a handle on this unprecedented access to your toxic ex. Since social media companies aren't going to limit access for you, it is up to you to take proactive and preemptive steps to make sure that you aren't tempted.

Research shows that limiting access to your drug of choice absolutely works, and is a good strategy to help you break your addiction.

In the classic delayed-gratification study where children were asked to resist eating one marshmallow in the moment so they could get more marshmallows later, many children resisted temptation by limiting access. They covered their eyes, tugged on their hair, turned the marshmallow into a toy to play with, or distracted themselves by kicking the desk (16). They knew that if they gave themselves access to that marshmallow, they would eat it and not get the better reward fifteen minutes later.

So, how exactly do you limit access to someone toxic that you're addicted to? I'm going to explain some practical ways to do this.

If you are currently with a toxic partner, limiting access will obviously be nearly impossible. So, this section is mainly for people addicted to an ex.

I'll start by addressing blocking them on social media. I'm not a big fan of blocking someone on social media as a tool to hurt them (like when couples fight and one blocks the other as a form of the "silent treatment"), but blocking someone so you're not tempted to engage them is a very powerful tool. In addition to blocking them, you can also block their friends, family, or anyone else whose posts may tempt or trigger you.

If blocking is too extreme for you, you can choose options to not see triggering content. On Facebook, you can remain friends, but "unfollow" people. On other apps, you can choose who shows up on your feed, and who doesn't.

There are also apps and programs that allow you to block access to distracting and addicting apps and websites of your choosing.

You may also consider changing your phone number if they reach out to you using that number.

Also, keep items that remind you of them out of sight. If you don't want to get rid of things because you have a sentimental attachment to them, store them away where you won't see them. Lock them up and give someone else the key.

Avoid any offline triggers as well. If you know they frequent a certain restaurant or bar, then go to other places to eat and drink. If you drive by their house on the way to work, choose a different route.

If your friends and family bring them up in conversations, ask them to please refrain from doing that.

Also, I suggest disengaging from internet groups, influencers, YouTube channels and other platforms that consistently keep you triggered about your ex. A lot of social media content reinforces feelings of anger, sadness, and victimhood, and can keep you constantly triggered about your toxic ex.

So, the more you limit access to your toxic ex, the easier it will be to move on and create the new life that you want.

Chapter 26

Saying "No" and Basic Boundaries

Most clients I work with who end up with toxic people struggle with two core issues: people-pleasing and overthinking. If you struggle with these two issues, you will have real trouble setting boundaries and saying "no" when needed. In this chapter, I want to explain how to say "no" so that you feel good and affirm your boundaries.

It is beyond the scope of this book to get into a lot of detail about boundaries (perhaps in a future book!), but this chapter will provide some basics to help you say "no" to your toxic ex or partner.

I want to mention first that whenever asserting any boundary, *make sure you are in a position of safety.* Setting boundaries when you are in a position of danger or potential abuse can be dangerous. So, what I am writing in this chapter applies to you if you are safe. If you are *not* safe, please contact law enforcement or get to a position of safety.

I am a natural people-pleaser and overthinker. When I was in college, a married couple at church wanted my brother and me to listen to a tape of a long sermon by a minister they liked. We wanted to do other things, and kept putting it off.

Rather than just telling them we didn't have time, weren't a huge fan of that minister, or that we didn't get around to it, we just kept avoiding them (so brave, I know!).

Finally, one time they brought it up around us, and I courageously looked the other way and made Jonathan field the conversation.

He stumbled over his words and half-heartedly said he listened to it. He then had to fake his way through a conversation about it for the next few minutes. I'm grateful he took one for the team!

This is what ends up happening when you can't say "no" or establish your boundaries. You end up doing things you don't want to do, being inauthentic, and in some cases, putting yourself in harm's way.

Many people in toxic relationships have lost years of their lives, thousands of dollars, and put themselves and their children in harm's way because of their inability to say "no."

The easiest way to say "no" is to just say "no." You do not owe anyone a reason if you say "no." I would say "full stop," but as a people-pleaser, I know this is easier said than done.

I know that many of you are, like me, polite and empathetic, and want more creative ways to say "no" if you are asked to do something by someone toxic.

So, here are a few strategies that can help you say "no" when someone makes a request of you.

The first step is to empathize with them. You can even empathize with someone toxic that you're addicted to. You don't have to give into them or believe they are a good person, but you can still empathize with them.

This step is important, because when you make someone feel heard, it can disarm them and help them accept the "no" more easily.

To do this, just start your "no" statement with "I know you…" and try to figure out the need they have that is motivating them to ask something of you.

"I know you're bored tonight and need something to do…"

"I know you are really busy and picking up our kids can be a challenge…"

"I know you have been struggling financially lately…"

Step two is to add "but I..." and provide a *reason* why you can't do something. Believe it or not, research shows that just adding a reason, even if it's not a good one, makes your statement more persuasive (17).

So, let's continue the examples from above.

"I know you're bored tonight and need something to do, but I told you I'm not interested in hanging out anymore."

"I know you are really busy and picking up our kids can be a challenge, but I'm at work right now and you committed to picking them up."

"I know you have been struggling financially lately, but I am not comfortable giving you the money."

Finally, if you want, you can add a suggestion that might help them get the need they have met. For example:

"I know you're bored tonight and need something to do, but I told you I'm not interested in hanging out anymore. I saw John was out at the local club, so can't you hang out with him?"

"I know you are really busy and picking up our kids can be a challenge, but I'm at work right now and you committed to picking them up. Have you tried asking your mom to pick them up?"

"I know you have been struggling financially lately, but I am not comfortable giving you the money. Can you get extra hours at work?"

Note that the "padding" on these examples is designed to make saying "no" feel better for you and persuade them to accept your answer. It is not meant to somehow "give in" to the toxic person.

Like I said earlier, all you owe someone is a "no." Even then, unless you are required to respond for some reason, simply ignoring them is also perfectly fine.

Remember that once you have said "no," especially if you have added the extras I mentioned above, you are under no obligation to explain yourself further.

If you wish to, remember to keep reinforcing the "no" consistently and simply, and do *not* get into the weeds they will likely try to draw you into.

Toxic people often persist and utilize different manipulation tactics the longer you don't give into them (see "Appendix A" for some of these tactics).

Keep this in mind. They may do anything they can to get their way, much like a toddler would.

I had a friend whose ex threatened her, apologetically cried to her, and threatened to end his life, all in a matter of minutes, during a conversation when she was refusing to allow him to visit her.

Remember that two things fuel them and keep them going: strong emotional reactions and when you give into them.

Learning to state your "no" persistently and calmly, and back it up by not responding further if needed, is the best way to break the cycle of reactivity that you have with them. If you do this, you will simultaneously lessen your emotional addiction to them and convey your "no" with strength and courage.

Chapter 27

This Too Shall Pass

When we are in the middle of craving something, or in this case, someone, the craving seems very intense and real. Our brain is telling us that we *must* give in and indulge the craving.

But the reality is that the craving isn't going to last forever. Depending on what you are craving, it could dissipate within a few minutes, or perhaps last up to 30 minutes. And, even then, the intensity often is not steady, and increases and decreases throughout this time (18, 19).

Waiting out a craving is an important aspect of handling it. Giving the craving time to pass seems so simple, but a lot of people reject it in part because it is so simple (and because the craving seems so real in the moment).

If you have ever given up a habit (like smoking or overeating), and now you rarely have cravings, you know how well this works. It's just that when a craving is fresh and you're used to giving in, your brain is going to tell you that you have "no choice" but to give in.

If you feel a craving coming on, find something to do that keeps your mind (and body, if possible, like exercise) occupied. You can even use "The 7-Step Creation Protocol" to direct your awareness away from your craving and to something else.

Another technique is to, in that moment, count backwards from 25 to 0, including halves expressed as decimals. So, for example, 25, 24.5, 24, and so forth. Don't write it out. Make your brain do it without a written aid.

This will accomplish two things. It will allow time to pass and direct your brain's energy to your frontal lobe, which is required to process the decimals. This directs energy away from your limbic brain, deactivating the parts of your brain where the craving is flaring up. If you're particularly good at counting down by halves, then try it with thirds or quarters, or try skipping a number to make it more difficult.

Calling up a friend can also be helpful. Educate them in advance about how they can provide support. My friends and I use this process whenever we feel tempted to reach out to someone who is bad for us.

First, let your friend know that you are sincerely trying to give up contact with someone toxic. Let them know that it is addictive, and you may need to contact them occasionally to distract you from a craving, or support you when it gets really bad.

Second, when you call them, be honest that you are struggling, and that you need them to talk you through it for a few minutes. I have had friends call me up and say, "David, you know the drill. My brain is sending me a temptation to contact my ex, so please remind me why that's a bad idea."

I promise you that your friends and family will be happy to spend a few minutes helping you resist a craving for someone toxic. That is preferable to them having to spend hours and days dealing with the chaotic aftermath if you give in and engage your toxic ex.

If you are a friend or family member of someone who is addicted to a toxic person, offering to help them when they are having a craving can be very supportive. Just let them know they can contact you anytime.

Try this out today. When you get a craving, find ways to distract yourself for some time while the craving passes, or use the countdown method I gave you.

As you do this, pay attention to the sensation of the craving, and notice that it weakens as time passes.

Contact a friend or loved one for support, and enjoy the

support you are getting.

Give it enough time to pass, and you'll see that you aren't controlled by your cravings.

Chapter 28

The "Unnamed Clothing Company Text Test"

Many of my clients, when they first come to see me, believe they are fully over their toxic ex. They say this while they vent about them, constantly post on social media about them, and are regularly triggered by them. They talk about them any chance they get, and even make life decisions based on them.

This is one of the nefarious things about being in relationships with toxic people. Years and even decades after the relationship ends, they often still exert undue control over their victims.

They may not exert it directly, but they do so by taking up a lot of mental space in the minds of their victims.

When I work with clients, my goal is not for them to hate their toxic ex, but rather to view them neutrally. If you understand how the brain works, the opposite of love is *not* hate as seems intuitive. It is neutrality.

As I mentioned previously, research shows that the neural pathways of strong romantic love and strong hate overlap significantly. They are two sides of the same neurological coin, and many people who spent their mental energy obsessively and unhealthily "loving" a toxic person will simply switch to spending their mental energy obsessively and unhealthily hating them.

When they "loved" them, they gave all their time to them, focused on them, and were emotionally controlled by them. Now that they hate them, they do the same things.

If they see their ex in public, they immediately get angry, or sad, or post something passive-aggressive on social media. If they find out their ex is dating someone new, they will call up their friends and discuss it for hours. They may spend hours analyzing their ex's behavior or waste lots of text discussing their ex on social media.

Do you see my point? Many people behave the *exact same way* toward their ex as they did before; they just label this unhealthy obsession as "hate" rather than "love."

So, you may be wondering, "what the heck is the 'Unnamed Clothing Company Text Test?'" Great question! Let me explain.

When I first wrote this book, I had an actual clothing company in the name of this test. It's a popular clothing company, and I wear many of their clothes. However, in the interest of not running afoul of corporate lawyers trained to send cease-and-desist letters, I decided to instead just call this the "Unnamed Clothing Company Text Test."

Honestly, I find this name more hilarious than the original, which will make it even more memorable, so you'll think about it more often. And, if you want to abbreviate it, the abbreviation is even just as funny to say: "UCCTT."

I guess I still haven't explained what it means…so here goes. While I like this clothing company, they send me texts about their deals and products every so often. One day when one came in, I was looking for a good analogy for being neutral to an ex, and it came to me.

This company's texts really don't make me feel much of anything. I may check them, or I may not. When they come in, I neither get excited, nor do I get angry about them. I largely ignore them, and I am mostly neutral towards them. I'll check out the deals if I really need clothes, but I usually don't. Basically, I barely notice them and never strongly react to them one way or the other.

If you can react this way to your ex, then you are truly on the path to being "over" them. Think about the content you see on social media that you ignore, or all the information throughout the day that you just don't care much about. You ignore or barely react to most things.

The things that "get under your skin" and you pay attention to are that way because you have a strong emotional attachment to something related to them.

When something gets under your skin, that can lead to reactivity and feeling emotions that lead you to do disempowering things.

I like the analogy "getting under your skin" because when that happens, that thing controls you. When your ex "gets under your skin" and sends you down the path of reactivity, it is truly like they have possessed you, and are overtaking your body and mind.

This is why "The 7-Step Creation Protocol" can be so useful. If you find yourself going down the usual path of reactivity, you can focus on going down another path. In this case, it is the path of neutrality.

If you work the healing process, and rewire your brain, you'll find that you will start to feel more and more neutral towards your ex. In other words, they will become more and more irrelevant, like so many emails and texts you just ignore.

You will start to give your mental energy and time to things that matter, like improving your physical health, pursuing your dreams, seeing your friends, and even making new ones.

As you do this, you may even meet someone you want to get to know romantically, and rather than talking about your past ex frequently, you'll be talking about your present and future with this new, healthy person.

The more you do this, the less you'll care about your ex. As you work the healing process, keep this phrase in mind: "aim for irrelevance."

If you do, the more you'll be able to pass the "Unnamed Clothing Company Text Test," and the more you are moving toward feelings of irrelevance toward your ex.

I started this book with a lot of "bad news" and that included some client stories. The good news is that every one of the clients I referenced moved significantly closer to making their exes irrelevant, and they ended up reclaiming their lives.

Chapter 29

What About Dating?

When working with clients, those who are addicted to someone toxic are tempted to take two extremes regarding future dating.

Many try to find someone to replace their toxic ex almost immediately, desperately seeking someone new they can become addicted to. Getting back into the dating "scene" is simply them trying to find someone else to give them the dopamine fix they are missing that their ex provided.

Others, however, disappear from the dating scene for a very long period, convinced they are worthless, or that relationships are so scary, they are best avoided, even if they do deep-down want to find someone to connect with.

Ultimately, I believe that neither extreme is very healthy and helpful, and I'll provide some guidance on this matter in this chapter.

One main reason that you have ended up in toxic relationships is likely that you have jumped quickly from one relationship to another. When you are feeling lonely, isolated, and worthless, after being with someone toxic (or if you were dumped), your limbic brain is going to desperately want you to jump into another relationship quickly to make those feelings go away.

While this is the "easier" path, it isn't the best path. Because, when you're feeling horrible and vulnerable, you're particularly susceptible to being taken in by toxic people, because they will often quickly and freely say the loving things that you so desperately want to hear. This is often called "love bombing." It is also a common tactic of romance scammers who steal money from people. Please check out "Appendix A" for a glossary of common manipulation tactics.

So, rushing back into dating is not a good idea when you haven't properly healed from your addiction, especially if you are looking for a relationship eventually. Even if you aren't looking for a relationship, but maybe just want to "test the waters," it is still very easy to get hooked on someone toxic while you're in a vulnerable state.

However, isolating yourself from relationships isn't healthy either, especially if you're still interested in being romantically involved with someone.

So how do you maintain the balance? Unfortunately, there is no hard and fast rule. In some instances, you may be ready to move on quickly, and in other cases, you may benefit from waiting a few months or even years if your life is a complete mess in need of genuine healing.

I suggest focusing on healing for at least three to six months before you start to date, especially if you have rarely, if ever, been single as an adult or teenager. Let me repeat this: if you have rarely been single, it is very important for you to be single for a while.

I guarantee if you have rarely been single, you consider relationships to be the "solution" to your problems, and you are using relationships to feel complete and whole, which will always have disastrous consequences.

Some people will disagree with me and say that I am suggesting you wait too long, while others will say my recommendation is too short. Ultimately, it depends on how proactively you focus on healing.

When it comes to dating again, one principle to remember is S-L-O-W D-O-W-N.

Notice how I really emphasized this? Virtually everyone I know who is addicted to someone toxic moved very quickly with that person. They jumped into dating quickly. They fell in love quickly. They got intimate quickly. They wanted to be in a relationship quickly. They merged finances quickly and moved in together quickly. They got married quickly. They planned a future quickly.

When you move this quickly, your brain is in the infatuation state I discussed in detail earlier in the book. And, not only are you missing red flags, but you're making commitments in this altered state that will be hard to undo later (marriage licenses are much cheaper than divorces!).

So, slow down.

Take your time getting back into the dating scene. Enjoy being single and focus on healing.

Take your time wanting a relationship: get to know the person as a friend first. This will filter out a lot of toxic people who are using you for a good time (a good time for them anyway).

Take your time getting sexually intimate, because it will also filter out people who are just wanting sex. It will also help keep your brain from beginning the pair-bonding process before you have a chance to determine if they are a good person.

Take your time with relationship milestones. You don't have to be engaged within a year. You don't have to get married immediately. This desperation to achieve milestones quickly is a result of your "in love" brain chemistry, and in some cases, even your insecurity and attachment issues. It also could be a toxic person's way of controlling you if they insist on doing these things quickly.

Take your time merging finances or moving in together. If they need money immediately, it's not your responsibility to "float them." If they need a place to stay, let them find one that is within their budget, by themselves. And, enjoy living separately for a while so you can get to know them before you share a lease.

Slowing down will also allow you to complete the healing process fully. You'll never be fully healed because none of us are perfect, but here is a good way to know if you are sufficiently healed. Once you reach a point where you feel whole and complete enough that you don't *need* a relationship, and you can survive and thrive as a single person, then you are paradoxically ready to be in a relationship.

The best relationships are those where two people who don't need each other come together voluntarily to enjoy life together. When you reach a point where you are happy and content without a partner, that is when you are likely ready to find a new relationship.

Chapter 30

Gratitude

When you're in survival mode, it's common to believe that your life is awful and there is no way you can ever achieve anything, like I mentioned when I discussed the "confidence-accomplishment spiral."

Survival mode trains us to see everything in a dark and negative way. And, when we see the world this way, it impacts what we believe, feel, and do.

One client of mine believed she was incapable of ever meeting a great man. She told me her life was a mess, and that she could never turn it around to the point where she could reasonably get a date with someone decent.

When she described her life, it was interesting. She was

accomplished in many ways, her guy friends clearly wanted to date her, and she was nice and friendly. Yet, to hear her describe her life, it was the opposite. She believed she had nothing going for her, that she was unattractive, and that her personality was repulsive.

When I work with clients they often "delete" the positive from their life, choosing instead to pay attention to the negative. Their brains have so focused on surviving for years and decades, that they now are keenly aware of negatives, but by doing this, they have made themselves unaware of positives.

This may be something you struggle with as well. One answer to this is gratitude.

Research on gratitude is fascinating. Gratitude has been shown to improve your mood, help you sleep, and boost immunity. It also reduces depression and anxiety, and can help with chronic pain (20).

I believe this is because gratitude causes you to focus on what's going right rather than what is going wrong. Now, I'm not saying to ignore what is going wrong. Most of us are acutely aware of the handful of things that are going wrong. But, we take for granted the hundreds, and even thousands, of things in our lives that are going right.

Let me give you an example that I have used on social media. I know people who can be driving a very nice car through a beautiful neighborhood. As they drive, colorful flowers are blooming everywhere, while they're listening to their choice of millions of songs, and are they focused on those things? No, they are in the middle of a text fight with someone, or thinking about something negative someone said to them an hour ago!

This just shows you how easy it is to delete the positives and focus on the negatives.

Gratitude allows you to acknowledge the good and positives in your life, which will help you feel better, and take more positive actions.

One way to take advantage of the benefits of gratitude is to keep a gratitude journal. Or you can just vocalize your gratitude to yourself, but also others.

Upon waking, I express my gratitude for five things, even if they are simple things like my bed or electricity flowing through the wires in my house. Before bed, I do the same. At bed, I think of things that happened throughout the day.

I also make it a point to express my gratitude to others, rather than taking people for granted, although I'm not perfect at this, of course.

Expressing your gratitude to others for what they have done, or who they are to you, not only makes you feel better, but it makes others feel better.

Finally, you can express your gratitude for things that may

seem difficult at the moment. For example, you can express gratitude for a difficulty that is helping you develop courage or become a better person.

Using gratitude will help you make positive changes, and help you become a healed, balanced person who thinks more about good things in your life, and less about your toxic ex or partner.

Chapter 31

Future Deeper Work Part 1: Time, Support, and Integration

Healing doesn't happen overnight, especially if you have endured years of trauma from being in a toxic relationship. The issue is complicated because many people are driven into toxic relationships because of childhood and adolescent issues.

In other words, the process of healing isn't instantaneous. We often wish it were quick and easy. We want to jump through the healing process to get to the end, so we can avoid the pain and difficulty that come with healing.

Healing requires time and intention and will involve setbacks. It can be aided by things like therapy, coaching, hypnosis, support, and accountability. No book can provide these elements.

This is why this book is just the beginning, and not the end. But just be aware that if you work the healing process, you will find that it is an amazing endeavor.

Let me outline a few things that will help you on your journey to heal from your addiction to a toxic person, or how you can help others heal more deeply, if you are a healer or loved one.

Time

Changing brain wiring, resetting dysfunctional dopamine systems, and restoring balance in your life take time. It took a while to mess things up, so it may take some time to get things back in order. The longer you have let things slide, the more time and sacrifice may be needed to get back on track.

Just as you must let time pass for a craving to go away, time is an important part of healing and changing your brain wiring.

Support

When I was struggling with relationship issues, my friends and family helped me get through the worst. Actively seeking support from others can be very helpful in the healing process. By "active" I mean asking for help and support when needed.

Just let your close friends know that you are working the healing process, and that you would appreciate their support, but also honesty with you as you work through things.

Give them permission to stop you if you spend too much time venting or draining them emotionally. See if they can support you while you balance out your life, and make sure you are there for them in the same capacities you expect them to be there for you.

My friends and I don't keep score, but we know that we are both willing to give and take.

Integration

As a hypnotist, I believe an important part of healing is the integration of your conscious and unconscious minds. It is about bringing unconscious realities to light, including the parts that we may not want to admit (called "the shadow" in Jungian psychology), and then directing them with the conscious mind.

It is about developing an integrated self and using the vast resources of your unconscious mind without being controlled by the unconscious mind, particularly the shadow.

In terms of the brain, it is about accepting and guiding the older parts of your brain to achieve the goals of your frontal lobe.

Much of the work in this book has been about doing this, and you have even done "shadow" work, by owning and accepting the things you did, and do, that you regret. By bringing these unpleasant realities to light, you can direct them rather than be controlled by them.

So, integration is about being fully honest and authentic with yourself and others. Integration in this way is necessary to move past someone toxic and genuinely heal.

It will also help you stand up for your ethics and morals, and not be as controlled by your unconscious impulses. This can give you the strength to resist being constantly "smitten," simply because someone is passionate, charming, and attractive.

In the next chapter, I'm going to explain yet another way to do some deeper work.

CHAPTER 32

FUTURE DEEPER WORK PART 2: LETTING GO

There is a quote attributed to the Buddha that says "holding onto anger is like drinking poison and expecting the other person to die."

When you have been deeply hurt by someone toxic, it seems so natural to hold onto anger, resentment, and jealousy forever. Even the thought of letting go and forgiving them in any capacity may seem absurd, and you may be feeling automatic sensations of anger right now simply because I raised this possibility.

I'm not advocating immediate forgiveness or denying your anger. I'm certainly not suggesting you ever let someone toxic back into your life, even a little. However, I do believe that if you are ready for it, "letting go" and even beginning to forgive in some capacity will change your life.

I included this as part of the "future deeper work" section of this book, because letting go is simultaneously the most powerful thing you can do to heal, but also the most difficult. You may not be ready to do this, or even begin to consider it, and that is okay.

Throughout this book, I've explained how deeply hating your toxic partner or ex can be a sign of addiction in the same way deeply loving them can be. Hopefully you now realize this.

As the Buddha-attributed quote states, filling your head with anger and resentment often impacts you way more than the person you're directing them towards.

A family acquaintance named Rick held a grudge against his ex-wife for 30 years. Whenever you'd be around him, he would still talk about what happened 30 years prior.

Everyone else had forgotten about that and moved on. Nobody else on the planet cared about a dispute that happened in a small town in 1973. Everyone was focused on other things. But, not Rick. He had been drinking poison for 30 years, and it showed in his demeanor, appearance, and social life. He was lonely and angry, and he sabotaged many potential relationships because of this.

If your head is filled with constant thoughts of rage and revenge, you will never pass the "Unnamed Clothing Company Text Test" and you'll never view your ex neutrally.

You may think that holding a grudge and even plotting constant revenge will make you feel so much better, but research shows that it doesn't.

One brain scan study found that when you get revenge, you feel amazingly good…but only very briefly in the moment. However, in the long term, this isn't the case.

In the long run, revenge makes you feel worse, and prolongs the unpleasantness of the original offense (21). This may be why after taking revenge or expressing your anger and rage, you wake up the next day feeling pretty much the same way you felt the day before. If anything, you may feel the need to express even more anger.

When I work with clients, they often tell me that if they "let go" or even begin to forgive their toxic ex, they will be letting them "off the hook." While I never pressure anyone to let go or forgive someone, I do gently remind clients that forgiving isn't about letting the other person off the hook. It's about letting *you* off the hook.

Let's expand the fishing analogy behind the phrase "letting someone off the hook."

Imagine a fish dangling on a hook. The fish is squirming, thrashing, scared, upset, and angry. Now, think of who is really "on the hook" when you are constantly filled with anger and rage toward your ex, and harboring revenge fantasies.

Is your ex sitting around feeling that way? Probably not! While you're angry and thinking of them constantly, they are likely feeling just fine and have moved on. They aren't tortured…you are.

And, even if you seek revenge and make them feel anger and rage, does that lessen your anger and rage? As I pointed out, research shows that it doesn't. So, even if you get the best possible revenge, you are still "on the hook," feeling horrible.

Maybe this is why many major religions focus on the power of forgiveness and letting go, even to an extreme degree. It's not just Buddhists who believe this. The words of Jesus in "The Sermon on The Mount" echo this same principle. Jesus said, "if you forgive others for their sins, your heavenly Father will forgive you. But, if you refuse to forgive others of their sins, your Father will not forgive your sins" (22).

Perhaps, you're worried that letting go may mean you will go back to old habits, or that your toxic ex will not face necessary consequences for their behavior. Keep in mind that letting go, or even beginning to forgive, does *not* mean:

- Letting them back into your life.

- Allowing them to get out of any legal consequences or agreements related to you or others.

- Compromising any boundaries that you have established.

- Minimizing what they did to you.

- Hanging around them or being friendly to them.

- Acknowledging that your toxic ex is a good person or that you approve of their behavior.

Letting go simply means that you are freeing yourself from the attachments you have to them, so your thoughts, feelings, and actions can be directed toward living an amazing life on your terms.

If you must think in terms of revenge, this is by far the best "revenge" you can get anyway, because if it's one thing toxic people hate, it's when they are ignored and irrelevant.

The more you use the tools in this book, like "The 7-Step Creation Protocol," the more you'll naturally just feel like letting go, and you'll experience the peace and empowerment that comes with it.

Chapter 33

Hoping For The Best

Before I wrap the book up, I want to discuss *hope*. It's something that I hope (pun intended) you are beginning to feel more of since you have made your way through this book.

Hope is the fuel of dreams and ambitions. I know that may sound cheesy and corny, but when someone has hope, this is translated into motivation and action. When someone lacks hope, they almost invariably remain stuck, unmotivated, and don't do much.

If you think about classic movies and books, the protagonist, the hero, often has hope when nobody else does. They believe when everyone else doubts, and make things happen to overcome insurmountable odds that are stacked against them.

Great examples are Andy Dufresne in <u>The Shawshank Redemption</u> and Katniss Everdeen in <u>The Hunger Games</u>, both characters in books made into movies. Despite being placed in the most difficult of situations, their hope allowed them to see a way forward and move toward it.

While you may not be imprisoned unjustly or find yourself in a dystopian society where your friends and family are chosen at random to fight in brutal games for the pleasure of the super wealthy, you can benefit from hope as well.

Hope has been found to be associated with improved coping, increased well-being, and engagement in healthy behaviors among those going through chronic illnesses and issues. Hope is also protective against depression and suicide.

Among teens who have been studied, hope is linked with health, quality of life, self-esteem, and a sense of purpose (and it is likely the case for adults as well).

It has been identified as an essential factor in developing both maturity and resilience (23).

In one study, hope was found to be related to post-traumatic growth in parents of children with cancer, with more hope resulting in greater post-traumatic growth. Post-traumatic growth is defined in that study as "a positive change in values and major life goals experienced as a result of the struggle with a highly challenging life circumstance."

In plain English, this means that if you have hope, you're able to better process your trauma, find meaning in it, and change your life positively from the traumatic experience (24).

This is contrasted with people who stay stuck in their trauma, experience the continued negative effects of it, and have a lower quality of life due to this. You'll notice that this book is all about post-traumatic growth even though I haven't used the phrase until now.

So, what exactly is hope? Researcher Charles Snyder and colleagues came up with "Hope Theory." Their research focuses on two elements of hope: *pathways* and *agency* (25).

I'll briefly explain them, and you'll notice how in this book I have been helping you cultivate hope, perhaps even at moments when you didn't believe it was possible.

The first metric, "pathways," means that you must see a path forward to where you want to go. You have to be able to not just imagine a better future, but imagine the path forward to achieve that future. Throughout this book, I've given you resources to see your new path through time that will allow you to generate hope.

By quieting your limbic brain and using your frontal lobe to see the path forward, you're cultivating hope, which then motivates you to take that path.

The second metric, "agency," is that you must believe that your effort plays a role in bringing about the results. In other words, you must see with your own eyes that your actions can and will make a difference in achieving your goal. So, you need to experience "wins" along the way for you to have hope.

Sound familiar? The "confidence-accomplishment spiral" is going to help you cultivate hope, even if you didn't know it was doing that.

If you have gotten anything from this book, I hope that it is hope. Yes, that pun was intended, but roll with it. You can laugh and relax now, because you finally have hope.

I'll end this chapter with dialog from <u>The Shawshank Redemption</u> movie. Andy Dufresne, the innocent main character, just got out of solitary confinement after being there for a week, and is having a discussion with other inmates, including "Red." The inmates are amazed he made it that long in solitary without going insane.

Andy: "There's something inside that they can't get to, that they can't touch. It's yours."

Red: "What are you talking about?"

Andy: "Hope."

Chapter 34

Putting It All Together

I hope you enjoyed this book and can use the information and strategies within it to break your addiction to someone toxic. If you are a healer or loved one reading this, I hope that it can help you help others.

As I mentioned previously, it is important for you to *take action*. Do something that you learned here. Taking even a few minutes of authentic, healthy action is going to be significantly more effective than knowing every fact about toxic relationships in the world.

So, we are excited that now you are filled with contagious hope and you can begin creating the new you and the new reality that you want, one in which your toxic ex or partner is soon becoming just a neutral memory.

If you enjoyed this book, and it has helped change your life in some way, I'd be grateful if you would check out some of my other resources, books, and social media accounts. My brother and I also work directly with clients in a variety of areas, individually and in groups, if that is something that interests you. For more information, check out the end sections of this book.

To sign up for our email newsletter, where we provide you with updates and resources related to the content in this book, please visit the link that follows. When we release the companion workbook to this book, we will let you know immediately using that newsletter.

To subscribe: https://bit.ly/addictionsubscription.

Appendix A

Glossary Of Toxic Manipulation Tactics

In this Appendix, I want to provide you with some common manipulation techniques that toxic people often use, to not only hook you in, but also to continue getting your attention even after you have ended things.

This list isn't exhaustive, but should help you navigate tactics someone might use. This list should be helpful in dealing with someone toxic, but it also serves as a list of things to watch out for if you are getting back into dating.

I am not a big fan of "buzz words," and many of these terms can be overused and misapplied, sometimes frequently on social media. Nonetheless, they are real tactics to watch out for.

Also, if you find yourself using these tactics in relationships, then it is a good idea to continue healing and growing as a person.

Ambiguity: This is being intentionally vague or non-committal to keep others off-balance or to evade responsibility. They may use this when speaking about commitment or exclusivity.

Example: "I am interested in commitment at some point, you know that, but only when the time is right."

Bait and Switch: This is a tactic where the manipulator initially falsely appears a certain way, or promises certain things, but then drops the veneer, or goes back on their promises.

Example: They started out the relationship emphasizing how religious they were, and how important monogamy was. A year later, they never attend church and are pressuring you to "open" your relationship.

Catastrophizing: This involves making a mountain out of a molehill, or always focusing on the worst possible outcome to control others through fear or worry.

Example: "You didn't text me for an hour at work. You were probably hanging out with that new guy and cheating with him! I don't want you to talk to him again."

Damning With Faint Praise: This is a "backhanded compliment," when someone offers a seemingly positive comment or compliment that is intended to subtly criticize or undermine the other person.

Example: "The Thanksgiving dinner you made is so good, it's surprising! It's way better than what you normally cook."

Deflection: This is when the toxic person changes the subject or question to divert attention from their actions, often turning the focus onto the other person's perceived shortcomings.

Example: You are confronting them for cheating on you, and they bring up a time that you told a small lie a few years ago.

Denial: This is a refusal to acknowledge the impact of their negative behavior. It's a way for toxic individuals to avoid responsibility and continue their harmful actions without consequences.

Example: "I don't need to get help. Sure, I have issues keeping control of my temper from time-to-time, but everyone is like that."

Divide and Conquer: This tactic involves causing rifts between people or groups to weaken them and make it easier to manipulate them.

Example: They will create drama and issues between you and your friends and family, especially if they know that your friends and family don't like them.

Double Bind: This is when a person presents only two options for resolution, trapping the recipient. Whichever route the recipient chooses, they are in the wrong, providing the manipulator with control and power.

Example: You didn't do anything wrong, but your toxic partner says, "you can admit you're wrong or I'm not talking to you for the rest of the night."

Emotional Cheating: This refers to a situation where a person in a committed relationship develops a strong emotional bond or connection with someone else that they are obviously attracted to. This is a manipulation tactic because many toxic people will establish this type of relationship and claim there is nothing wrong with it since they aren't (yet) physically cheating.

Example: They spend more and more time with an attractive work "friend," even texting constantly outside of work. They tell their work "friend" more about their life than they tell you. They even complain about you to this person. When you confront them about this, they deny that it is even cheating.

Fake Apologies and Promises: Toxic people often provide apologies and promises to change, even though they know this likely won't happen. An apology is fake if it is never followed up with any sort of action.

Example: They profusely apologize for losing their cool and screaming at you, and say they will get help, but you have heard this same "song and dance" for years.

False Equivalence: Drawing a false comparison between two things, which can't be compared, to justify their behavior or perspective.

Example: They overslept from being high on marijuana and missed a major job interview. They explain that you "can't say anything" because you have used marijuana a few times in the past.

Fear, Obligation, and Guilt (FOG): Toxic people often use fear, obligation, and guilt as tools to manipulate and control others. They instill fear, make the person feel obligated, or use guilt to manipulate the person into doing what they want.

Example: "You're leaving me now? When we met you promised we'd be together forever! If you're okay with going back on your promises, then fine, leave!"

Flying Monkeys: These are the creatures the Wicked Witch of the West sends out to harass Dorothy in <u>The Wizard of Oz</u>. "Flying monkeys" are people convinced or coerced into doing a manipulator's bidding. They may be used to manipulate victims by gathering information, spreading rumors or lies, or intimidating or harassing them.

Example: Your toxic ex sends in one of their friends to your workplace to "innocently" talk to you, but their friend reports everything you said to your toxic ex.

Forced Team: The manipulator creates a sense of us-versus-them, forcing the person to take sides. Toxic people will often use this to keep you isolated from others.

Example: They will frame isolating you from friends and family as a "team" thing, where it's just you two versus everyone else, and nobody "gets" your relationship but you two.

Future Faking: This is when a person lies about the future to get what they want in the present. They will promise amazing things like a great future where you are married or even something simple like how they will pay you back all the money they owe you, when they get that amazing job their third cousin, twice removed, promised them.

Example: Said on a first date to get you comfortable so you'll have sex: "I see myself getting married again someday for sure. I'm honestly looking for someone just like you."

Gaslighting: This is where a person attempts to make another person question their own perceptions, memory, or sanity by repeatedly denying or distorting reality. This term comes from the 1944 film <u>Gaslight</u>, where a husband uses such tactics to make his wife believe she is losing her mind.

Example: You clearly know they said "I'll hurt you if you do this again," but later they just outright deny it, or claim they obviously didn't mean it literally and you're confused.

Guilt-Tripping: This involves making someone feel guilty, to manipulate them into behaving a certain way. It is a way of using a person's feelings of guilt to control and manipulate their actions.

Example: "Fine, don't respond to my text. You're just like all the other people in my life who always abandon me and never listen."

Hobby Stopping: To isolate you, toxic people will often get you to stop doing your hobbies, or other things that keep your life balanced, like going out in public to do things. This includes things that may make you desirable to others, like exercising.

Example: "Why do you always go to the gym? You know other guys are looking at you! You can work out at home."

Hoovering: Named after the Hoover vacuum, this term refers to the tactic of sucking people back into a toxic relationship with false promises of change, often after a period of no or minimal contact, trying to pull the person back in with kind gestures.

Example: After a few months of "no contact," you get a text from your toxic ex saying they have thought about everything, and how sorry they are. They even offer to take you to dinner.

Invalidation: This tactic involves dismissing or undermining a person's feelings, thoughts, or experiences to disorient them and establish dominance.

Example: "You think I'm out of control? Are you dumb or something? Jeez, you're always acting so stupid like a child."

Isolation: A toxic individual may try to cut you off from friends and family, to control the narrative or your actions without outside influence. They will often do this subtly using guilt-tripping, and make you feel bad if you do things without them. Or they will try to turn you against others.

Example: "I have been feeling sick lately, and have been struggling mentally today, and you want to go hang out with your friends, knowing I can't come! I am sorry, but that is selfish. Is a concert really more important than me?"

Jekyll and Hyde Behavior: This is when your partner or ex has unpredictable and volatile shifts in behavior. This delivers intermittent rewards and punishments which can establish an addictive trauma bond.

Example: When they come home from work, some days they are friendly, and cheerfully offer to make dinner. Other days they fly off the handle and yell and scream at you when you don't have dinner ready.

Love Bombing: This is when someone overwhelms you with affection, compliments, pet names, and promises for the future, which are designed to make you feel amazing, usually quickly after meeting. The sudden attention can be intoxicating, and cause you to overlook their undesirable traits. Romance scammers often use this tactic.

Example: (said within a few weeks of dating) "Baby, I'm really starting to believe that you're 'the one' because you're so beautiful and amazing. I never feel this way about people this quickly, but you just overwhelm me."

Moving the Goalposts: This is when the manipulator changes their demands or expectations once you have met them, effectively meaning you can never satisfy their demands.

Example: "Yes, you allow me to live rent free at your place, but you know I'm broke, and you're still asking me to pay for my own groceries. That's not what a good partner does."

Needy Entitlement: This is when the toxic person may have genuine needs, but they are entitled about it, and expect you to meet their needs in an excessive way.

Example: "You're cutting me off financially? You know I have a learning disability and can't understand money like you do. And this economy sucks! I told you I can look for a job when things improve."

Neglect: Deliberate lack of care or attention.

Example: Many partners refuse to contribute financially or emotionally to a relationship.

Passive-Aggressiveness: Expressing negative feelings indirectly rather than openly addressing them, often done in a way to subtly manipulate the situation.

Example: They are clearly upset with you, but instead of telling you why, they pout, and then later they post something on social media that is clearly directed toward you, or they gossip about you to a co-worker.

Playing the Victim: This is when the manipulator portrays themselves as the victim, to gain sympathy, and therefore control you because you feel sorry for them.

Example: "You know I had a bad childhood, which is why I get angry and put my hands on you. I try hard baby, but you know what I've been through, so I just can't change quickly."

Projection: This is when the manipulator projects their own thoughts, feelings, or expectations onto you. They accuse you of their own negative behaviors or emotions.

Example: Many cheaters accuse their partners of cheating. They may accuse you of never listening to them because they never listen.

Silent Treatment: This is when they intentionally ignore or exclude someone else as a form of punishment, because they know these actions hurt and bother the victim. This is different from setting a clear boundary of "no contact" or asking for some time to cool down before continuing a conversation.

Example: Your partner and you had a disagreement. In the middle of the discussion, they retreat into their bedroom and don't come out. They even block you on social media.

Smear Campaign: This is when a manipulator spreads false or damaging information about someone to undermine them, ruin their reputation, and isolate them.

Example: Your toxic ex has been telling all their co-workers that you cheated on them, which is why you both are separated, even though that isn't true; they cheated on you.

Stonewalling: This involves refusing to communicate or cooperate. The toxic person might ignore requests, refuse to answer questions, or shut down conversations, leaving the other person feeling frustrated and powerless. Again, this is different from establishing "no contact" or requesting a period to cool down before communicating.

Example: You share custody of your child with your ex, and you need to know what time to pick up them up, but your ex intentionally doesn't get back to you quickly enough for you to pick them up on time.

Threatening To Harm You, Themselves, or Others: This is when they tell you that if you do something that they don't like, they will hurt you, themselves, or someone else. This is one of the vilest tactics they can use, especially when they make you feel horrible because they may harm themselves. They often will pair this tactic with the excuse that they have mental health issues, which is a type of "playing the victim."

Example: "If you leave me, life won't be worth living anymore, and you'll miss me when I'm gone. You know I have mental health issues and can't handle you doing this!"

Triangulation: This is a tactic where the toxic person brings another person into the dynamic, making it a metaphorical triangle. They may do this to create insecurity, validate their actions, or stir up competition for their attention. This can include "hitting on" someone to make you feel jealous, drawing your family into a dispute, or even manipulating a therapist to take their side.

Example: Your partner is sharing your relationship problems with a co-worker. The co-worker is taking an interest in your partner, and when you confront the co-worker, the co-worker lectures you about your relationship problems.

Victim Blaming: Manipulators often shift the blame onto the victim for their abusive behaviors.

Example: Toxic people may say that you deserved to be cheated on because you may not have given them enough sexual attention, or because you were busy working a lot. Or, they may say that you deserved to receive their abuse because you stood up to them or went against a certain religious teaching.

Appendix B

Who We Are

My twin brother Jonathan and I are identical twins, hypnotists, and coaches. Together we operate Bennett Twins Hypnosis and Coaching.

I (David) have been active in business and media for over ten years. I have a popular TikTok channel, with over 120k followers. I create self-help and self-growth content that has been viewed over 40 million times by people all over the world.

I've been used as a trusted source in nearly 500 articles for various outlets, including appearances in Reader's Digest, Men's Health, Prevention Magazine, and The Boston Globe.

I've appeared on various radio and TV shows, including on 610 WTVN and WBNS 10-TV.

I graduated magna cum laude from Ohio University with a Bachelor of Arts in Psychology. While there I was inducted into the prestigious honor society Phi Beta Kappa, as well as Psi Chi, the honor society in Psychology. I also graduated summa cum laude from Emory University with a master's degree.

I'm fully certified in hypnosis, EFT, and coaching, with hundreds of hours of training and continuing education.

I was a high school teacher for ten years and worked as an executive at a counseling agency for six years. While there, I took courses related to addiction and various therapeutic interventions, including Cognitive-Behavioral Therapy, Dialectical-Behavioral Therapy, and Motivational Interviewing. In 2022, I started running my hypnosis, coaching, and social media business full-time.

My journey to where I am now began in 2008, when I met my friend and fellow hypnotist Joshua Wagner. Soon after we met, he, my brother, and I developed various behavioral "models" as foundations for personal and relationship success, many of which I use in my hypnosis and coaching practice, and some of which appear in this book.

I've worked with many clients over the last 10 years, and helped them change their lives through weight loss, leaving toxic partners, healing from the past, giving up bad habits, overcoming fears, and much more.

I love to read, write, exercise, and attend music festivals. I can be found running 5K races, half-marathons, and obstacle course races like The Tough Mudder. I also love coffee and seeing my friends, family, girlfriend Megan, and cat Coconut.

My brother Jonathan not only looks like me, but also has a similar background. He is an author, influencer, personal coach, hypnotist, and business owner. With over 120k followers and 3.5 million likes, he is popular on TikTok where he produces self-help content.

His insights have appeared in numerous publications, including Psychology Today, The New York Times, and The Wall Street Journal.

He has a bachelor's degree from Ohio University and a master's degree from Emory University. He is a member of the Phi Beta Kappa honor society.

He is certified in hypnosis, EFT, relationship coaching, and neuro-linguistic programming with hundreds of hours of training and continuing education. He is a member of the National Association of Transpersonal Hypnotherapists (NATH).

He has over ten years of teaching experience at the high school and university levels. He was formerly the CEO of a mid-sized non-profit counseling agency.

As a coach and hypnotist, he has assisted many clients in changing their lives, helping them lose weight, leave toxic partners, give up bad habits, heal from past pain, gain confidence and social skills, and embark on journeys of discovery and growth.

In his free time, he likes to read, write, run, lift weights, and play old school video games. He enjoys going to concerts, music festivals, riding roller coasters, traveling, and spending time with his daughter.

In the photo below, David is on the right, and Jonathan on the left.

APPENDIX C

MORE SUPPORT AND RESOURCES

We have many resources to help you heal and move beyond your addiction to someone toxic. These include books, audio workshops, and our social media channels where we regularly post empowering content.

We also work with clients one-on-one, and in group support environments. You can learn more about all of this by checking out the resources that follow.

If you benefitted from this book, and want to support us, we would be grateful if you checked out our other products. More are on the way, including a companion workbook. To order an item, or learn more, please scan the QR code next to each text.

Audio Courses

<u>Get Over Your Addiction to A Toxic Ex Or Partner Workshop</u>:

This course contains audio content that is similar to what is in this book, but in a helpful mp3 format that you can listen to while you drive or workout.

It also includes bonus hypnosis and meditation tracks.

Books

<u>Say It Like You Mean It: How To Use Affirmations and Declarations to Create The Life You Want</u>

This book explains how to write and use affirmations to rewire your brain and make significant changes. Affirmations change the way you speak to yourself, and this book will help you rewire your brain to embrace a new future, and new possibilities.

The book is a perfect companion to this one.

The Art of Hypnotic Manifestation: Mastering The Law Of Attraction For Personal Transformation Using Hypnotic Tools And Principles

In this book, we explain how to finally manifest the dream life that you want, using the principles and tools of hypnosis. This book will help you make even deeper changes necessary to create the life you have always wanted. If you enjoyed the tools in the book you're now reading, you'll love what you read in The Art of Hypnotic Manifestation.

From Red Flags To Real Love: A Strategic Guide To Avoid Duds and Find Someone Amazing

If you're thinking about dating again, but you're stuck in a pattern of choosing the wrong partners, this book will revolutionize your love life by helping you sort through duds, time wasters, and toxic people.

Lose Weight And Be Healthy Now: Forty Science-Based Weight Loss Tips to Transform Your Life

Jonathan and I both lost 50 lbs and kept it off for over 10 years. In this book, we share many of the tips, tricks, and mindset shifts that helped us do this in a healthy and sustained way.

Many people in toxic relationships have let their health slide and gained excessive weight. If you are at the point in the healing process where you want to explore losing weight, then check out this book.

Sign Up For Our Newsletter

To get regular updates from us, and to be the first to know about special products and deals, including the release of the upcoming companion workbook, please access the QR code beside this text, or visit: https://bit.ly/addictionsubscription.

Social Media and Website

These are sites where you can connect with us on social media. These sites also contain information about contacting us, booking a session, or working with us in other ways.

Bennett Twins Hypnosis and Coaching: BennettTwins.Com

David's Direct.Me: direct.me/dtbennett

David's TikTok: dtbennett

David's Instagram: dtbennett

Jonathan's Direct.Me: direct.me/jbennett

Jonathan's TikTok: jrbennett96

Jonathan's Instagram: jrbennett96

APPENDIX D

REFERENCES

Introduction

1. Earp, Brian, et al. "Addicted to Love: What Is Love Addiction and when Should It Be Treated?" <u>Philosophy, Psychiatry, & Psychology : PPP</u>, vol. 24, no. 1, 2017, p. 77, https://doi.org/10.1353/ppp.2017.0011. Accessed 10 May 2023.

Chapter 5

2. https://my.clevelandclinic.org/health/diseases/9742-narcissistic-personality-disorder

3. Campbell, W. Keith. <u>The New Science of Narcissism the New</u>

Science of Narcissism: Understanding One of the Greatest Psychological Challenges of Our Time-and What You Can Do about It. Sounds True, 2020.

Chapter 6

4. https://www.thecut.com/2017/02/why-heartbreak-getting-dumped-feel-so-bad.html

5. https://www.independent.co.uk/news/science/scientists-prove-it-really-is-a-thin-line-between-love-and-hate-976901.html

Chapter 9

6. https://www.newscientist.com/article/dn4957-hormones-converge-for-couples-in-love/

7. https://www.healthline.com/health-news/heres-how-much-weight-you-gain-during-relationships

8. Young, Larry, and Brian Alexander. The Chemistry between Us: Love, Sex, and the Science of Attraction. Current, 2004.

9. Marazziti, D., et al. "Alteration of the Platelet Serotonin

Transporter in Romantic Love." Psychological Medicine, vol. 29, no. 3, 1999, pp. 741–745, doi:10.1017/s0033291798007946.

Chapter 10

10. Champagne, Frances A., et al. "Variations in Maternal Care in the Rat as a Mediating Influence for the Effects of Environment on Development." Physiology & Behavior, vol. 79, no. 3, 2003, pp. 359–371, doi:10.1016/s0031-9384(03)00149-5.

11. https://www.nytimes.com/2011/01/11/science/11hormone.html

Chapter 11

12. https://feelingishealing.co.uk/intermittent-reinforcement/

Chapter 19

13. https://www.ulm.edu/~palmer/TheBiochemistryofStatusandtheFunctionofMoodStates.htm

Chapter 20

14. https://studyfinds.org/men-high-testosterone-cheat/

Chapter 22

15. Lieberman, Daniel Z. *Spellbound: Modern Science, Ancient Magic, and the Hidden Potential of the Unconscious Mind*. BenBella Books, 2022.

Chapter 25

16. Lembke, Anna. *Dopamine Nation: Finding Balance in the Age of Indulgence*. Dutton, 2023.

Chapter 26

17. Cialdini, Robert B. *Influence, New and Expanded: The Psychology of Persuasion*. HarperBusiness, 2021.

Chapter 27

18. https://diet.mayoclinic.org/us/blog/2021/beat-your-cravings-8-effective-techniques/

19. https://www.healthline.com/health/alcohol-cravings

Chapter 30

20. https://www.mayoclinichealthsystem.org/hometown-

health/speaking-of-health/can-expressing-gratitude-improve-health

Chapter 32

21. https://www.scienceofpeople.com/the-psychology-of-revenge/

22. <u>Matthew</u> 6:14-15 (my modern rendering based on <u>The King James Version</u> of the Bible)

Chapter 33

23. https://www.health.harvard.edu/blog/hope-why-it-matters-202107162547

24. Hullmann, Stephanie E., et al. "Posttraumatic Growth and Hope in Parents of Children with Cancer." <u>Journal of Psychosocial Oncology</u>, vol. 32, no. 6, 2014, pp. 696–707, doi:10.1080/07347332.2014.955241

25. https://www.psychologytoday.com/us/blog/beautiful-minds/201112/the-will-and-ways-hope

Made in the USA
Monee, IL
11 December 2023

48833852R00152